Commercial Contracts for Managers Series

THE MANAGERS GUIDE TO UNDERSTANDING TENDERS

Also available in the ***Commercial Contracts for Managers Series***:

- *Understanding Commercial Contract Negotiation*
- *Understanding Commonly Used Contract Terms*
- *Understanding Confidentiality Agreements*
- *Understanding Indemnity Clauses*

Commercial Contracts for Managers Series

THE MANAGERS GUIDE TO UNDERSTANDING TENDERS

by

Frank Adoranti

Dip Law (BAB), MBA (UNE), FCIS

Solicitor and Barrister of the Supreme Court of New South Wales

Chartered Secretary

Notary Public

LES50NS PROFESSIONAL PUBLISHING

First published in Great Britain. 2006

LES5ONS PROFESSIONAL PUBLISHING Limited
A Division of LES5ONS (PUBLISHING) Limited
Fitzroy House
11 Chenies Street
London WC1E 7EY, United Kingdom

Email: info@fiftylessons.com

ISBN 0-85297-761-1

Cover Designer: Insignia Graphics

Senior Editor: Jessica Perini

Printed by Loupe Solutions

PREFACE

Just because you've been signing contracts for years, it doesn't mean you have understood what you've been signing.

One of management's biggest fears is that of an employee exposing the company to the risk of potentially ruinous litigation. It is a fear with genuine foundation.

The cost of litigation is measured in the billions (indeed one estimate is that in the USA alone, the cost is in excess of $200 billion).

A company exposed to litigation suffers the following consequences:

- uncertainty;
- adverse publicity and loss of reputation; and
- expense and drain of management time.

These consequences are the natural enemies of the-manager. They undermine the marketplace's perception of the company and can also have adverse effects on a company's share price. This is especially so given the post-Enron/Arthur Andersen climate of business.

During the last five years, I have devoted much time and effort to instilling a culture of litigation prevention in corporations, by the education of managers in fundamental concepts of commercial contracts.

A common question raised by managers at the conclusion of my seminars is: *What book can I read as a ready reference?* Unfortunately, I found no particular book catering to these aspects of corporate legal education. The most common problems expressed to me regarding existing books on the market were that they were:

- **too difficult to read:** the bulk of titles on the market dealing with contracts are scholarly academic works intended for the practising lawyer or law student;
- **not practical:** the less imposing and shorter "guides" are predominantly aimed at law students "cramming" or revising for examinations or oriented to consumer law issues (neighbourhood disputes, family law, wills and personal bankruptcy); and
- **not portable:** none are presented as handy reference guides specifically tailored to managers. They are usually off-putting in their size, length and/or prohibitive expense.

When discussing the concept of a managers' guide to commercial contracts, most of the comments I received from managers can be summarised in the following quotation:

> *Whilst it might not offer the depth of information on a particular topic that a textbook does, a handy guide in your briefcase accessible when you need it is far better than the volumes sitting on a shelf back at your home or office.*

This provided me with the final impetus to fill the need in this area. You hold in your hands the third in a series of books catering to this requirement.

Many organisations gain much of their new business from tendering and contract evaluations, which are (for many of them) an everyday occurrence.

To the non-lawyer, tender documents and contracts (like many legal documents) are often shrouded in mystery. The documents are becoming increasingly unwieldy as they attempt to weave complex structures of rules and protocols. This is especially so as contracts tend to outsource more risk to Contractors and cater for a large number of contingencies.

The purpose of this book is to provide an explanation of the function and operation of tenders, as well as clear demonstrations illustrating the effects of the attempts to outsource sometimes disproportionate amounts of risk to Contractors. The aim is to help managers understand such issues and ultimately avoid the aggravation of contract disputes and litigation.

We will commence with a brief foundation of the tendering process and the basic flow of a typical tendering transaction. In so doing, the reader will gain an understanding of the reasons behind concepts such as terminating a contract for convenience and the inclusion of liquidated damages clauses in such contracts.

Along the way, you will find a number of practical tips on some of the traps and pitfalls of tendering and contract evaluation.

As a safeguard, you should *always* seek qualified legal advice in specific situations.

When dealing with the law, often, there is no single "right" answer. This series of books will help managers develop the ability to deal with particular aspects of the ambiguities of contracts. They should be of assistance to every manager dealing with commercial contracts and agreements and from sales and business development staff through to the CEO and CFO. The series caters to those in large publicly-listed organisations as well as to smaller businesses.

In writing this series, I have drawn on my 16-years of experience in the law in various countries. I have tried to cut through the mire of theory and "legalese" and distil the essence of a highly technical topic into something easily understandable and digestible for the manager in a hurry.

Where possible, I have used actual examples, taken from situations I have encountered, as illustrations of many of the points made in the book. The names, identities and particular circumstances have, of course, been changed in order to protect the confidentiality of those persons and entities.

I trust you find this series of guides as useful to read as I found them enjoyable to write.

FRANK ADORANTI

Sydney, March 2006

ACKNOWLEDGMENTS

Naturally, a work which is the product of many years of research and development never comes together single-handedly.

I offer my sincere thanks to Glen O'Connor for the most useful and incisive review comments on the manuscript. To Warwick Isherwood, I am grateful for the benefit of his expertise in providing me with extensive review commentary and other ideas to further improve the usefulness and practicality of the work. Thanks also to Graham Wilkinson for reviewing the CAPEX and working capital sections and for the helpful comments.

I am also grateful to Maddocks Lawyers of Melbourne for their kind assistance with the sample conditions of tender in Appendix D and for their permission to reproduce the statutory declaration in Appendix E.

To my editor, Jessica Perini, who has put herself through a third book with me, I once again thank you for your keen eye, good humour and continued encouragement throughout the, often arduous (and seemingly endless), journey.

To my brother Gino for his friendship and support.

To my parents, for their total love and support; they will always be my treasures.

To Kiara, Gianni and Luca — collectively, our greatest source of laughter, fun and good times.

Finally, to my wife Rosalie, for her unwavering belief over the many years this project has taken to come to fruition. She will always be the centre of my universe and brilliant mother to our incredibly delightful (and increasingly mischievous) children.

ABOUT THE AUTHOR

The author has worked in the private practice of law since 1986. Since 1996 he has worked with a number of multinational corporations both in Europe and in the Asia–Pacific region.

As an international corporate lawyer and consultant, he has reviewed thousands of significant commercial agreements and has seen, first hand, the damage that organisations suffer when proper care is not exercised in negotiating and correctly documenting contract terms. He has also conducted and managed hundreds of millions of dollars of litigation in various parts of the world, caused by such lack of care.

For many years, major tenders and contract evaluations have been a daily (and very often, nightly) part of his life.

He has been involved in a broad range of commercial transactions ranging from the acquisition and sale of international companies to simple confidentiality agreements, and much else in between. He has also assisted organisations with:

- mergers and acquisitions;
- post-merger integrations;
- corporate restructures;
- establishment of tender and bidding processes;
- crisis management planning;
- contract management systems;
- legal audit and legal risk assessments;
- relations with external lawyers;
- planning corporate legal departments;
- compliance programs; and
- in-house training programs and seminars on contracts and other legal issues.

In addition to his qualifications as a lawyer, he has an MBA and is a Fellow of the Institute of Chartered Secretaries and Administrators. He is also a Notary Public.

TABLE OF CONTENTS

Chapter 6 Other isssues in tendering

Chapter 7 Conclusion

INTRODUCTION

This book is dedicated to demystifying the tendering process. It will give managers and employees a broad understanding of the contractual side of the process as well as the many potential pitfalls that await the prospective tenderer. In so doing, we will also examine aspects of the contract evaluation process, which will give managers and employees an understanding of how organisations review and evaluate contracts in the course of business. The information contained in this section is not merely confined to tendering situations, is also equally applicable to contract reviews.

You will learn a number of different ways that an organisation can create or streamline a tendering processes so that it becomes systematised. As the book unfolds, the reader will begin to understand how the proper management of the process is essential.

Not all managers understand the nuances of tender documents, their accompanying rules and contract documents. Indeed, some have been encountering them for many years, sometimes without an appreciation of their full significance and potential ramifications.

For many organisations, tendering is the very foundation of their operations and revenue stream. For this reason, it is important that organisations involved in tendering have an understanding of the various options available to them and of the best ways to select the most appropriate ones suited to their philosophies and needs.

The current climate of business is one of heightened awareness of risk and of continued attempts to outsource and transfer such risk, wherever possible.

Failure to detect attempts to unfairly transfer risk, or miscalculations in tenders or contract evaluations, can have a lasting impact — not only for many years *during* the life of a contract, but, more significantly, for many years *after* the expiry or termination of the term of the contract.

Directors and managers must ensure that adequate processes and systems are in place to ensure that a balance is achieved between winning new business and capitalising on new opportunities and not inadvertently committing an organisation to unduly onerous provisions or accepting an inordinately high level of risk.

Such processes will also help prevent an organisation from inadvertently "wandering off course" into non-core activities.

> ***Golden Rule***
>
> In tenders, ***preventative*** measures and safeguards are the best tools available.
>
> Once you have committed to an unduly onerous contract that has not been properly scrutinised, it is often too late to renegotiate.
>
> You cannot "unring" the proverbial bell.

Neither directors nor managers wish to be exposed to personal liability for having committed their company to a major loss-making contract, or one that lacked basic and necessary safeguards. Worse still would be the case where valuable proprietary rights were actually surrendered or even *given* away.

Depending upon the gravity of such an unfortunate act or omission, litigation could potentially follow from several quarters, almost certainly from shareholders or investors.

Good corporate governance requires that corporations implement proactive programmes and strategies with emphasis on proper contract evaluation and scrutiny in the first place, rather than going into "damage control" after the event.

These factors combine to make a fundamental understanding of tendering procedures and contract evaluation more relevant than ever.

We will commence by going back to the very basics and explaining why the tendering process is commonly used and what the general objectives are of a Principal seeking expressions of interest via the tendering process. Through the use of examples, we will see the differences between the competing methods that organisations employ in the evaluation of contracts.

Some of the key steps that organisations must follow when involved in a tendering process will be highlighted.

We will then focus on a number of different and significant contract clauses and issues that recur in tendering documentation. For example, some of the things we will look at are liquidated damages, assignment and change of control clauses, *force majeure*, indemnities and dispute resolution issues.

Chapter 1

FOUNDATION

Introduction

In most jurisdictions, probity rules and regulations usually provide that government contract work must be open to tender. Tendering is also becoming increasingly common in the private sector.

The reason being that in the selection of Contractors, most organisations wish to have procedures that will *generate sufficient competitive forces* to:

- allow them to obtain the best price/quality mix;
- allow them to obtain the best value for money;
- provide the best and most efficient solution; and
- ensure probity, fairness and transparency in the selection process.

According to Nobel Prize winning economist Frederik Hayek:

> *The market price cannot be known until there is competition.*

Governments are primary users of tendering processes. Indeed, government contracting is a multi-billion dollar business. As governments spend taxpayers' dollars, it is imperative that they not only act in the most appropriate manner but also be *seen* to be acting that way.

From the Principal's perspective, once there has been a decision made to acquire particular goods and services, there is an often overwhelming desire to "get it done". After the decision is actually made to proceed, all other intermediate steps may tend to be seen as an impediment to obtaining that result. Yet, if the process is not handled correctly, the whole thing becomes a disaster that all parties may come to regret.

In the United States and in Europe there are specialised systems regulating government tenders.

A number of levels of government tenders in Australia are subject to various tendering protocols and regulation of some kind. For example, in New South Wales, regulations under the *Local Government Act* establish a tendering code for local government agencies to follow. Also, state government procurement agencies are bound by competitive tendering policies and the Code of Tendering for the Construction Industry.

Australia does not have any such system governing private tenders.

■■■

Terminology

Before proceeding, we need to understand some basic terminology.

Tender

"Tender" can have one of two meanings, depending upon the context in which it is used.

When a Principal requires a certain product or service to be supplied, it might send out an invitation to other companies to provide competitive quotations for the work to be done. In this instance, the word "tender" refers to the tender *process* — whereby an invitation is issued by a Principal, seeking prospective tenderers to make an offer in accordance with the terms of the tender documents.

Or, it can otherwise be a reference to the *documents* (as in "the tender documents") containing the offer actually made by the tenderer to the Principal.

Tenderer (or Contractor) and the Principal

For ease of reference throughout the book, we will refer to the two main parties in a tender as follows:

1) **Principal** — the party requiring the provision of certain goods and/or services from a Contractor. The Principal will invite various Contractors to tender for the contract.

2) **Contractor** — the party who wishes to win the contract to provide the goods and/or services required by the Principal. The Contractor is the *tenderer* or *prospective tenderer*.

Conforming tender or **conforming bid**

This is a tender lodged in *complete* compliance with the conditions of tender, with *all* documents completed in the required format. Typically, the tender or bid must be an offer capable of acceptance in the form lodged and is sometimes required to remain open for acceptance for a fixed period of time (during which time, it cannot be withdrawn by the tenderer).

Whilst the tender documents may state that the bid may not be withdrawn, one might query whether it is legally possible to enforce this, given such factors as the questionable existence of adequate consideration etc.

Usually, in practice, if a bidder does not wish to proceed, then the bid may not (and probably should not) be accepted.

Furthermore, in relation to anything but the most minor of contracts, there are usually negotiations between the Contractor and the Principal before the documents are finally executed. The tender documents are almost never accepted on their face value.

Non-conforming tender or non-complying bid

This is a tender that does not comply with the conditions of tender and (depending upon those conditions) may be automatically disqualified from being considered as a valid tender. Sometimes, if the conditions of tender allow, non-conforming bids may still be considered, with the non-conformity simply being one of the evaluation criteria.

Expression of Interest (EOI)

An EOI is often a very short document whereby the Principal seeks to obtain a list of interested participants so that the Request for Tender (RFT) can be sent to certain Contractors on a selective basis. The EOI can sometimes be as rudimentary as the draft letter shown in Appendix A with the questionnaire set out in Appendix B attached.

Typically, in the case of larger tenders, a Principal will have conducted its own market research to ascertain a group of the firms most likely to have the capability of providing the required goods or services. At the conclusion of its research it would send to each of the firms a questionnaire seeking further details on products/services offered, geographical coverage, capacity to supply, financial and company structure information etc.

A sample of such a questionnaire is shown in Appendix B. Of course, not all of the information will be necessary or applicable in each particular case.

Request for Tender (RFT), Request for Proposal (RFP), or even Request for Quotation (RFQ)

Once all of the questionnaires issued by the Principal are received and processed, the number of prospective tenderers may have been narrowed down further. This might be due to the content of the responses or lack of appropriate interest.

The terms RFT, RFP or RFQ are used (interchangeably) to signify the stage in the process where interested parties have already put themselves forward to be qualified as prospective tenderers. Those so qualified by the Principal, are provided with the relevant tender documents, to enable them to participate in the tendering process.

The next step will consist of the issue of tender documents with (if appropriate) an appointment for the prospective tenderers to attend a presentation by the Principal to all tenderers.

Depending upon the nature of the tender (especially in major tenders), the documents distributed to qualified Contractors, inviting them to submit a bid, will usually consist of the Principal's background information, together with details of product and/or service requirements and specifications, quality system information, key performance indicators and the conditions of contract.

Tender documents

Tender documents — which are usually drawn together to form the final contract between the Principal and successful Contractor — will usually consist of:

- The formal invitation to tender, which includes the formal project name, reference number, deadline for the closing of tenders and address for lodgement of tenders.
- Conditions of the tendering process.
- Conditions of contract (these can sometimes be separate documents called "General Conditions" as well as "Special Conditions").
- Specifications which will define the nature of the goods and/or services required by the Principal to be provided by the Contractor selected as the successful tenderer.
- The format of response to be adopted by prospective tenderers, sometimes called the "tenderer's offer" form. This will often contain the checklist of completed documents required to be lodged to ensure the tender is a valid and conforming one. A sample of the tenderer's offer form is contained in Appendix C.

■■■

Stages of the tendering process

Figure 1 provides a broad picture of the typical stages in a tendering process.

FIGURE 1: STAGES IN A TENDERING PROCESS

Defining the objectives

- preparation of clear specifications
- statement of the requirements
- requirements for the particular goods and/or services sought are defined

Preparation of tender documents

Tender documents will usually consist of

- formal invitation to tender
- conditions of the tendering process
- conditions of contract
- specifications
- the format of response to be adopted by prospective tenderers

Expressions of interest

- advertising seeking expressions of interest
- parties register their interest
- evidence of tenderer's experience and financial standing sought

Request for tender

- suitably qualified Contractors provided with a set of tender documents and invited to submit tenders

Evaluation of tenders submitted

- tenders evaluated according to the pre-determined criteria
- the successful tenderer is selected

Award of the contract

- additional negotiations to "fine-tune" the relevant contract documentation
- execution of the documents by the parties

Management of the works
• monitoring of the works against criteria defined in the contract
Completion of the works
• further performance monitoring and final sign-off prior to final payments settled

■■■

Benefits of a tendering process or system

Most professional tendering organisations will have libraries of standard document templates and wording concerning their:

- history;
- track record and reputation;
- expertise;
- methodologies;
- systems;
- accreditations; and
- capabilities.

In the increasingly limited timeframes available in tenders, such organisations can produce professional and well-considered tender documentation with dazzling speed and brilliant accuracy.

The Principal's evaluation team (who see many poorly produced documents) will tend to be impressed with speed, clarity, accuracy and impeccable presentation.

■■■

Organisations without a tendering process

Two of the main difficulties arising in organisations without a tendering process or system are:

1) **Inconsistent approaches to tender bids.**
That is, a Contractor may make differing statements (or even conflicting ones) about its capabilities or its pricing might not adhere to organisational models, etc.

2) **An inadequate understanding of corporate requirements.**
Corporate requirements may include an organisation's policy on authority limits for capital expenditure sign-off. These limits might not be universally known or even properly applied throughout the Contractor's organisation. For example, a line manager may have a $250,000 limit of approval for any capital expenditure on a particular contract. Sometimes, managers may be tempted to exceed such a limit knowing they are not properly enforced.

Even allowing for this, such a manager may not be aware of a rigid internal requirement for a 25% return on capital expended (ROCE). It might only be discovered *after* the contract has been won that the financial models for the tender were based upon incorrect ROCE assumptions.

Unfortunately for some organisations, the "wake-up call" to implement a tender bidding system only comes *after* the tendering disaster — where an almost impossible contract loss is snatched from the jaws of victory by poor preparation and complacency.

Chapter 2

TENDER DOCUMENTS

In this chapter, we will concentrate on the three primary aspects of tender documents:

1) conditions of tender (see Appendix D for sample of conditions of tender);
2) conditions of contract; and
3) the "tenderer's offer" form (see Appendix B for a sample of a tenderer's offer form).

For our purposes, it will be assumed that the Principal will have satisfied itself in relation to the relevant aspects of financial standing and capability of the tenderer.

■■■

Conditions of tender

The "conditions of tender" are the conditions governing the tender process itself. They are separate and distinct from the conditions of the contract for the provision of the goods and/or services that are the subject of the tender.

The conditions of tender are of primary importance to the tenderer for three reasons:

1) they will govern whether the tender submitted will be an offer capable of acceptance and whether it is required to remain open for a certain period without the submitting party being able to withdraw it;

2) they will govern how a non-conforming bid will be considered (if at all) or treated; and

3) they will set forth the selection criteria for the evaluation of conforming tenders.

Appendix D contains a representative sample of conditions of tender.

Often, the conditions will be broadly drafted and will give wide discretionary powers for the selection and determination of the successful bid.

Indeed, it is common for there to be a clause

reserving the right to select any bid and not necessarily the one with the lowest price. A prudent Principal will reserve the right to not select any bid lodged and to terminate or suspend the tender process at any time.

On a practical note, if a Principal ever chose to exercise such a right, it would need to do so carefully in order to avoid any liability at common law or under any applicable Fair Trading or Unfair Trade Practices laws. If a Principal then sought to repeat the entire tendering process thereafter, the enthusiastic participation of Contractors might well be significantly diminished.

Such conditions preserve maximum flexibility for a Principal, to enable the tendering process to be changed or terminated due to changing necessities and requirements.

For a Contractor, the two primary "hooks" (but not the only ones) to be aware of are:

1) the non-conforming bid provision; and
2) the open offer provision.

Non-conforming bid provision

The non-conforming bid provision is a clause providing that any tender submission which does not accept the conditions of contract without amendment or challenge, will disqualify the tender submission. This means that the tender will not even be considered unless it accepts all of the contract terms without qualification or reservation.

One even more dangerous variation of this theme is a provision stating that submission of a tender bid constitutes the *unqualified acceptance* of the contract, forming part of the tender documents.

This means that if the Contractor is selected as the successful tenderer, it must sign and work to the contract terms *as they are*; there is no room for negotiation or variation, since they have been accepted in their current form.

Open offer provision

The open offer provision states that the tender must be an open offer capable of acceptance by the other party (the Principal) and must remain open for a period of X days, during which time it may not be withdrawn.

Obviously, this takes away any control or bargaining power from the tenderer and leaves the offer on the table for the period during which it must remain open. This could, in some circumstances, be quite dangerous to the tendering party.

If the offer is open for a long period of time, the

Contractor loses any control over the contract adjustments, in response to market forces (eg, price fluctuations), during the intervening period. That is, if labour and material prices rise steeply, such price increases may not be able to be passed on to the Principal and will have to be absorbed by the Contractor. This will, of course, change the entire viability of the contract from that originally forecast by the Contractor. At best, a contract becomes uneconomical; at worst, the consequences could prove to be a financial disaster to a Contractor.

Golden Rule

It is important that you pay careful attention to the conditions of tender, since the formal requirements for compliance are usually **non-negotiable.**

If even one of those requirements is missed, the entire tender could thereby become invalid and may not be considered.

As most tender submissions involve thousands of man-hours in their preparation, you do not want to be responsible for having a tender disqualified because of something simple — such as late delivery of the tender documents, documents with missing attachments or delivery of the tender documents to the incorrect address.

A Principal may face a significant risk of being found to have breached ordinary rules of probity if it allows a tender that does not comply with the formal requirements, to be considered.

If so, a Principal could expose itself to an action by the other tenderers.

Conditions of contract

This is the contract that will ultimately govern the relationship between the parties in the event that the tenderer is selected as the successful bidder.

As such, it is important that the Contractor subjects this document to careful scrutiny, to avoid years of pain, which could render the contract an unprofitable and disastrous one for the Contractor.

Some Contractors are unduly sensitive to objecting to any onerous terms of the contract, for fear of disqualifying themselves from consideration of their bids. This is the time for dialogue with the Principal to ascertain their attitude to a tenderer departing from the conditions of tender or the conditions of contract.

In the case of government tenders, this is usually best done openly in a tenderer's briefing session. A number of government tenders have a prescribed process of written questions and answers from each Contractor. Written responses to these questions and answers are then supplied to all Contractors. This is to ensure that probity is maintained and avoids the appearance of any one tenderer being favoured or unfairly assisted.

If this is done verbally during a meeting it is *imperative* to obtain such answer in writing, particularly where a departure from the written conditions is being permitted or encouraged.

As a rule, both the Principal and Contractors should view the briefing session as very important. It may give insights as to the way in which the Principal or Contractors (as the case may be) are thinking. It may also give an insight as to how the competitive Contractors might be preparing their tender. For this reason, a prudent Contractor might use the opportunity to freely question the Principal — although a Contractor needs to be careful to not reveal too much of its own strategy, in the process.

Variations to the conditions of contract

It is trite to say that any modifications to a contract should be recorded in writing. However, it bears repeating given that most tenders are dynamic and sometimes fast-moving processes.

Often there are many things happening within a compressed timeframe; preparation of the tender submissions, briefing sessions with the Principal and a multitude of internal Contractor meetings.

There may also be an interactive question and answer process with the Principal, proceeding simultaneously with other events.

Clarifications of the conditions of contract may be discussed openly with all prospective tenderers during the process. Alternatively, there may be an allowance of time made for the successful tenderer to negotiate specific terms of the contract.

Whatever the path to contract amendments, it is important that such amendments be recorded and agreed to in writing by both sides. This eliminates any doubt or uncertainty as to the precise nature of what was agreed and when.

Also, any corresponding adjustments to pricing or to the scope of works (triggered by such variations to the contract) should also be dealt with and agreed to in writing.

> **Golden Rule**
>
> Where a Principal agrees to vary any condition of tender or condition of contract, it is imperative that such agreement be obtained *in writing* from a duly authorised officer of the Principal.

■■■

"Tenderer's offer" form

The tenderer's offer form usually commences with words such as:

> *The tenderer hereby submits its bid for XXXX comprising the following documents.*

The form will list (sometimes in the form of a checklist) the various documents that together will comprise and form part of the Contractor's tender and offer to the Principal. The tenderer's offer form is the document tying everything together.

At the end of the form is usually a statement of agreement to be bound by the conditions of tender, followed by a section for execution by the organisation lodging the bid.

A sample of such a form can be found in Appendix C.

Assuming compliance with the conditions of tender, the Contractor makes an offer to the Principal from the time of submission of the tenderer's offer form (with the relevant bundle of documents attached). The Principal is free to accept the offer in the form submitted. Depending upon the particular conditions of tender, the offer must remain open for a certain period, during which, it cannot be withdrawn by the Contractor.

Some clever players will consider adding to their tenderer's offer form words to the effect that:

This tender is subject to board approval.

Such "cleverness" should be embarked upon with great care. Depending upon the wording of the conditions of tender, this could create a situation of non-compliance, potentially disqualifying the entire tender from consideration.

■ ■ ■

Confidentiality agreements

A confidentiality agreement may often be referred to as a *non-disclosure agreement* or *secrecy agreement*. The terms can be used interchangeably, however, for the sake of convenience, the term *confidentiality agreement* will be used here.

A confidentiality agreement is a binding contract between two (or sometimes more) individuals or entities whereby one party (typically the Principal, as the Discloser) agrees to provide the other (the Contractor, as the Recipient) with certain confidential information, which the Recipient agrees not to disclose or use, other than in the manner and for the limited purpose specified in the confidentiality agreement.

It also serves to provide for the orderly return or destruction of the confidential information supplied in the event that a deal between the parties does not ultimately proceed. The agreement usually sets out the obligations of the Contractor to safeguard the confidential information and details the remedies available in the event of a breach.

A Principal will often ask a prospective Contractor to execute a confidentiality agreement prior to providing the Contractor with a tender package. These tender packages may contain some sensitive information outlining the Principal's operations and requirements. A Principal needs to be certain — to the fullest extent possible — that their commercially sensitive information will only be used for a limited and specified purpose.

The Principal needs to consider the answers to at least the following questions:

- What information is to be considered confidential?
- For what specific purpose will the information be supplied?
- Are there to be any exceptions to what should be considered to be confidential information?
- Are there to be any permissible disclosures?

A prudent Contractor should also be asking itself the above questions in considering the issue and determining whether the Principal's request is indeed a fair one or whether it oversteps the bounds of what could be considered reasonable, in the circumstances.

An important confidentiality point for the Contractor is whether "novel" aspects of their tender bid can be used and shown to others by the Principal.

The Principal may wish to establish a "level playing field" by revealing novel aspects to other Contractors. If this occurs, the Contractor automatically loses one of its competitive edges as well as freely surrendering valuable intellectual property. This is particularly a matter of concern with large projects (such as public–private partnerships) where there is a concern of Contractors (especially in Australia) that this information will become public knowledge and they will lose their competitive advantage.

A prudent Contractor must ensure that its valuable intellectual property and competitive advantages are properly protected against wholesale and indiscriminate disclosure. **This is a vitally important step for a Contractor.**

For a more comprehensive discussion on confidentiality agreements and demonstrations of specific examples of their use, you should consult ***Understanding Confidentiality Agreements***, the second volume in the *Commercial Contracts for Managers Series*.

Chapter 3

TENDERING: THE STEPS

Following is a table of steps a Contractor might follow prior to submitting a quotation. Naturally, not *all* steps will apply to *all* Contractors. In some situations, there may be other additional steps not shown here. The checklist is intended as a general guide only.

Checklist: steps for prospective tenderers
☑ **Appoint a project co-ordinator for the bid**
☑ **Strategy** ☑ Is this contract a strategic fit for the Contractor? ☑ Does it represent the Contractor's core business or is it diversifying into other areas?
☑ **Scope of works** ☑ Is it clearly defined? ☑ Is it properly documented? ☑ Is it unequivocal or is there room for interpretation on the main issues? ☑ Can it be properly priced in its current form?

Checklist: steps for prospective tenderers — *continued*

- ☑ **Variations to scope**
  - ☑ Does the contract permit the Principal to vary the scope of the works?
  - ☑ Is the process of requiring variations clearly defined?
  - ☑ Is the scope of any variation work properly defined?
  - ☑ Is there an agreed mechanism for the pricing of variations?
  - ☑ Will the price mechanism for variations unfairly prejudice one of the parties?
  - ☑ Can the variations be rejected by the Contractor if pricing is either not agreed or proves disadvantageous to the Contractor?
- ☑ **Third Parties**
  - ☑ Are any third parties necessary to carry out any of the works? — ie, Partner, sub-contractors, third party suppliers, etc.
  - ☑ Are there any agreements that need to be put in place for such third parties? — eg, teaming agreements or joint venture agreements for joint bidders or sub-contracts for single bidders or supplier agreements for either joint or single bidders?
- ☑ **Insurance**
  - ☑ Is the Contractor's existing insurance coverage adequate when taking into account the contract works?
- ☑ **Capital expenditure (CAPEX)**
  - ☑ Is the amount within the Contractor's normal limits?
  - ☑ Are there specific return on capital employed (ROCE) requirements that the Contractor must deliver? In many organisations the ROCE requirement is about 15–20%.
  - ☑ Is the CAPEX amount able to be amortised over the life of the contract?
  - ☑ Is the CAPEX amount properly protected under the contract in the case of early termination?

Checklist: steps for prospective tenderers — *continued*

- ☑ Prepare a business case for the CAPEX required.
- ☑ At the end of the Contractor's term, is there a compulsory buy-back provision in the contract for the Principal or incoming Contractor?

☑ **Financial modelling — Do the numbers "stack up"?**

- ☑ Are cash flow and working capital requirements of the Contractor met?

☑ **Contract review — legal**

- ☑ Are there any contract terms or conditions of tender inconsistent with the Contractor's own terms?
- ☑ Is pricing fixed? Is there an adequate "rise and fall" provision?
- ☑ Liquidated damages. Are they capped?
- ☑ Indemnity clauses. Are there appropriate carve-outs? Is there an express exclusion of consequential loss and damage?
- ☑ Change of law provision. Who carries the risk?
- ☑ Change of control provision. Is this relevant to the Contractor's future plans? Is there any exclusion for internal reorganisation within the Contractor's own company group?
- ☑ Dispute resolution. Are the methods set forth appropriate for these parties in this contract?
- ☑ *Force majeure*. Are the *force majeure* events all covered? How will industrial disputes be dealt with?
- ☑ Are there any intellectual property rights that need to be dealt with?
- ☑ Are there any time of the essence obligations?
- ☑ Are the governing law and jurisdiction choices appropriate?
- ☑ Termination for convenience. Are demobilisation costs provided?
- ☑ Will there be any impact on other divisions or related companies of the Contractor?

Checklist: steps for prospective tenderers — *continued*

- ☑ Specialised provisions may need to be inserted in IT contracts — eg, escrow of source code, co-operation between Contractors and integration issues. The same applies to other specialised contract provisions, for example, construction contracts.

☑ **Amendments to contract**
- ☑ Discuss amendments with Principal.
- ☑ Any amendments or agreements to amend must be obtained in writing from an authorised officer of the Principal.

☑ **Are there opportunities to cross-sell?**

☑ **Occupational health and safety issues**

☑ **Environmental issues**

☑ **Senior management sign-off**

☑ **Sub-contractors**
- ☑ Secure commitment on same terms and conditions (back-to-back) as contract with Principal from sub-contractors and/or third party suppliers — subject to winning bid **and** signing of contracts.
- ☑ Ensure sub-contractors and/or third party suppliers have adequate insurance in place.

☑ **Proceed to quotation**
- ☑ Check correct address and closing date for submission of tender bid

☑ **Cross fingers and wait**

The above checklist is a guide to the steps a tenderer will take before lodging a bid. However, the final decision to proceed with a bid will generally be made on the basis of the *commercial viability equation* being satisfied. That is, the proposed Contractor will only want to bid on a contract that it considers will be profitable and a good strategic fit. The contract must be compatible with its core business and/or future direction.

On occasion, a decision may be made by the Contractor to expand into a different area of business. If so, some sacrifices on profitability could be made. If the contract is a particularly prestigious one, it could be taken on at a loss because of the strong referral potential for other new business.

Golden Rule

The commercial viability equation upon which the Contractor bases its decision to bid is:

Clear technical specifications +

Acceptable contract terms +

Financial criteria satisfied =

Commercial viability of a contract

Timing the evaluation of contracts

Some organisations are tempted to leave contract negotiations until after they have been awarded the contract. This should only be done where the conditions of tender permit it to be done. If so, the tender bid should expressly state this to be the case.

Consider a section in an organisation's tendering procedures' manual "Contract Review Procedures" which reads as follows:

> *Upon award of a contract, the contract shall be reviewed in accordance with Contract Processing Procedure to resolve any differences between the tender and the awarded contract.*

Unfortunately, by the time the contract is actually awarded, it can sometimes be too late to negotiate its terms.

In any business, it is important that an organisation not commit itself to contract terms that it has not fully considered.

Increasingly, companies are asking tenderers to commit to contract terms *in their bid documents.*

As tendering becomes a more competitive process, Principals will tend to capitalise on the competitive pressures exerted upon tenderers by the process itself. The inherent pressure generated is the reason why many Principals obtain far more favourable results from Contractors than could otherwise have been obtained by either individual negotiation or any other method.

One of the inherent pressures of the tendering process is the pressure upon a tenderer not to submit a tender that is non-compliant. Such pressure can often be augmented by insinuations or explicit statements to the effect that a bid's chances of success will decrease with any or a higher number of non-compliances.

Naturally, this places considerable pressure on the sales/business development staff of a Contractor in exercising their judgment. Sometimes, a borderline case may be allowed to pass unchecked in the quest to achieve success in winning the bid.

In many organisations, a sales team's success is judged only by the number of tender bids that it wins. This can create a conflict of interest situation. For a further examination of this topic, you should refer to **Inherent conflict of interest** in Chapter 5.

In the absence of express and unequivocal conditions permitting contract negotiations at a later time — when the competitive forces are lessened — the mere hope that the Principal's benevolence will allow this to happen, is a dangerous assumption by the Contractor. On many occasions, a successful tenderer has been compelled to accept a contract containing unreasonably onerous terms, simply because it has failed to pay attention to these principles. A more detailed examination of the procedure and systems for the evaluation of contracts takes place in Chapter 5.

Controls on the orderly flow of information

Often, in the rush of multiple enquiries and dealings with various prospective Contractors, Principals may lose sight of documents and material being handed over and to whom.

Control of documents can easily be lost. Importantly, if a Contractor is given a document, prior to tender submission, and the contents of that document change, but this has not been communicated to a Contractor, a Contractor may have a significant grievance against the Principal.

Situations may arise creating disputes and acrimony over what the Principal actually handed over and what the Contractor should, consequently, be returning and/or be obligated to maintain as confidential. This is particularly the case in relation to unsuccessful bidders. It is important that a Principal maintain a register or list of all information being provided to each prospective Contractor.

■■■

Rating a prospective Contractor

Once the bids have all been lodged by the tenderers, the Principal applies its pre-determined selection criteria to choose the successful bidder.

It must read through all bids with an eye on its selection priorities to understand how sensitive and responsive each bidder is to each of these. It must then apply a weighting to each of them, according to their importance to the Principal, to finally arrive at a "score" for each bidder.

Different criteria will carry a different weighting depending upon the level of their importance to the Principal.

Below is a generic list of criteria used by a Principal in selecting a successful tenderer. The list should be borne in mind by a Contractor from the pre-tendering stage.

Some clues will be available in the tender documentation, background information, question and answer sessions, as well from any presentations by the Principal.

A bid's chance of success can be dramatically increased by an astute Contractor's sensitivity to the Principal's material and significant criteria.

Note that some of the criteria may not be relevant to some Principals.

Checklist: assessment criteria for a prospective Contractor
☑ The financial strength and backing of the Contractor for the projected life of the contract
☑ Quality of verbal and written presentation
☑ Product range
☑ Assessment of Contractor personnel
☑ Logistics capabilities
☑ Quality systems and any certifications in place
☑ General reputation and customer references
☑ Invoicing
☑ Innovativeness of solutions put forward in the proposal
☑ Transparency
☑ Price competitiveness
☑ Flexibility of the Contractor and responsiveness to changes in the scope of works
☑ Contractor's partnering approach

The checklist does not and cannot show the weight carried by each criterion in the mind of the particular Principal. This is a subjective matter and will depend entirely upon:

- the individual circumstances of the Principal;
- the market; and
- the nature and type of works to be performed by the Contractor.

If a Contractor is made aware of the assessment criteria and those assessment criteria change (without appropriate notification thereof to the Contractor), this might then give rise to a legitimate grievance against the Principal by the Contractor.

■■■

Steps after winning a contract

The work of the tender team concludes at this stage, while the work of the organisation's implementation and operations teams begins.

The atmosphere can be one of celebration or relief at achieving such success. However, the next few steps are crucial. If mismanaged, they have the potential to undo all of the hard work up to this point.

The formal handover to the operations team should not be their first contact with the contract works. Ideally, they will have worked with the tender team and their cost estimators in the preparation of the bid. In this way, they will have been able to spot any operational hurdles at the contract evaluation stage, enabling appropriate queries to be made and necessary clarifications to be sought from the Principal.

Otherwise, there is a real risk that a specification that works well in theory, could prove unprofitable or unworkable in practice.

In large contracts, it may well mean that the tender team (or at least some of them) may need to become part of the operational team. A loss of the members of the tender team (by either the Principal or the Contractor) may create significant problems, at a later stage, for that party. Thus the Principal/Contractor needs to carefully consider the terms of employment of the tender team.

To ensure a smooth transition from award of contract to its implementation, the following is a list of the steps to be typically addressed.

Checklist: steps after award of contract

- ☑ Ensure the contract documentation (including the final scope of work, technical specifications and commercial terms) conforms to the Principal's offer and that all changes to the original contract and specifications are agreed and properly recorded in writing.
- ☑ Ensure that agreements with key suppliers are in place.
- ☑ Ensure that proper back-to-back agreements with sub-contractors are in place.
- ☑ Verify that insurance coverage required to be carried by Contractor is in place.
- ☑ Verify that all sub-contractors' insurance coverage is in place and that certificates of currency are obtained.
- ☑ Activate the implementation team.
- ☑ Formal handover to operations team.

Chapter 4

CONTRACT PROVISIONS

Outsourcing risk to Contractors

As companies become more risk-aware and risk-averse, the trend is to increase the outsourcing of risk to a Contractor. Often, in the push to do so, inequities arise in the fair apportionment of risk.

Increasingly, Principals conducting tenders are asking tenderers to commit to unduly onerous contract terms in their bid documents. There is increasing pressure on tenderers not to submit tenders that are *non-compliant*. The expression *non-compliant,* of course, referring to objections or issues raised by a Contractor in relation to the Principal's form of contract attached to the tender documentation.

A Principal might apply pressure to a prospective Contractor to accept the terms of the Principal's contract document without qualification or condition. Such pressure could take the form of hints, insinuations or explicit statements to the effect that a tender bid's chances of success will decrease with any (or a higher number of) non-compliances.

In the face of such pressure, a tenderer may be tempted to fall into the trap of:

> *Other companies will agree to these clauses, therefore, in order to be competitive, we must do the same.*

Succumbing to that temptation can sometimes lead to disaster.

Conversely, boundless savings can result to the company that has successfully outsourced such liability.

A Principal can employ a number of mechanisms to achieve such a transfer of risk. We will examine some of them in the following sections.

■■■

Indemnities

More often than not, a Principal will require a prospective Contractor to give an indemnity for any loss sustained by the Principal in the event of any breach of the contract by the Contractor.

An indemnity is a contractual commitment by a party to make good a specified loss suffered by the other party. In other words, it is an acknowledgment and promise by one party to cover the potential liability of another.

Such a clause typically reads as follows:

The Contractor shall indemnify and hold harmless the Principal (including but not limited to the Principal's officers, employees, contractors and agents) against all losses, damages, costs or expenses which the Principal incurs or may incur as a result of any act, omission, negligence or breach of this Agreement by the Contractor.

Notice the clause above does not contain restrictions or limits upon:

- the types of losses sustained by the Principal;
- whether the obligation to indemnify is limited only to direct losses sustained by the Principal;
- whether the obligation to indemnify extends to include indirect (or consequential) losses or otherwise;
- whether the obligation to indemnify arises only through the actions or inactions of the Contractor, or in combination with a third party.

A prudent Contractor would make the following modifications to the above clause (note that deleted words are shown as ~~strikethrough~~ text and added words are underlined):

> *The Contractor shall indemnify and hold harmless the Principal (including but not limited to the Principal's officers, employees, contractors and agents) against ~~all~~ losses, damages, costs or expenses which the Principal directly and reasonably incurs ~~or may incur~~ as a direct result of and to the extent of any act, omission, negligence or material breach of this Agreement by the Contractor in connection with or arising out of the performance of the Services. The Contractor's obligation to indemnify shall not extend to include any indirect or consequential loss.*

A key feature of an indemnity is that the obligation created by it can often extend *beyond* that which would otherwise be imposed on a party under the general law.

Typically, in a claim for a breach of contract against a Contractor, a Principal might not recover *all* of the loss incurred. The indemnity, however, will extend to cover losses that might not otherwise have been covered by a claim for damages for breach of the agreement. That is to say, in the event of a breach, the Contractor's damages' bill will generally be higher with an indemnity clause than without one.

For a Principal, the indemnity is a particularly attractive mechanism to outsource liability to a Contractor. This is because its very concept is to make the injured party whole again, as if the loss had not occurred, *even if the person who agrees to indemnify would not otherwise have had any obligation to do so*. This is particularly so in circumstances where it contains wording such as:

> *notwithstanding the negligence of the Principal or anyone acting under the Principal's authority*

or

> *shall include any indirect or consequential loss suffered by the Principal or anyone claiming through the Principal*

A prudent Contractor must be aware of a Principal's attempts to outsource liability *beyond* the scope of the goods and/or services to be provided by the Contractor.

Golden Rule

In a situation where a Contractor provides goods and/or services to a Principal, a typical indemnity clause will provide for the Contractor to indemnify the Principal against:

> *any damage, loss, cost, expense or liability incurred by the Principal arising out of:*
>
> *(a) the provision of the goods and/or services;*
>
> *(b) any breach of the agreement; or*
>
> *(c) any act, omission or negligence*
>
> *caused by the Contractor, its employees, agents or sub-contractors.*

It is vitally important to carefully check any indemnity clause in a contract with your lawyer. In addition, you should also check with your insurer, to ensure that you have in place appropriate and adequate insurance coverage against such losses.

For a more comprehensive discussion on indemnity clauses and a demonstration of specific examples of the use of such clauses, you should consult ***Understanding Indemnity Clauses***, the first volume in the *Commercial Contracts for Managers Series*.

Consequential loss

To reiterate, a "fair" indemnity clause does not seek to avoid a party's responsibility or liability for its actions. It merely seeks to limit the extent of liability to that which may be *directly* attributable to any negligence or wrongdoing.

The absence of a consequential loss provision, allows the company giving the indemnity to accurately identify and measure the extent and nature of potential losses. It can then more accurately quantify and manage its risk accordingly.

It can be argued that consequential loss clauses are not normal or reasonable commercial terms.

Normal loss is the loss suffered as a *direct* result of a breach or action. Whereas, consequential loss is the loss suffered because of *circumstances peculiar to a particular person or entity.*

It can, therefore, be argued that a clause allowing consequential damages to be claimed *would unfairly broaden and extend liability beyond the normal commercial realm.*

Consequential losses, by their nature, are uncertain and difficult to quantify. They involve the acceptance of responsibility for risks that are not foreseeable and not within the ordinary knowledge of the party giving the indemnity. In addition, they can in some circumstances even extend to include the losses of persons who are not parties to the agreement!

As with all things in the law, often the choices are not only restricted to either black or white. Compromise is an essential feature of successful negotiations over commercial contracts.

The choice confronting a party to a commercial contract might often be either to accept a consequential loss clause or not.

Alternatively, where a party has specific concerns relating to a *particular* event of consequential loss, it may be possible for the parties to direct their minds to dealing specifically and only with such an event, to attempt to find a mutually acceptable solution to the problem.

However, there may be situations in which the acceptance of consequential loss provisions is unavoidable. In some instances, one may be compelled by commercial considerations to accept a consequential loss clause. For example, an airline caterer would find it very difficult in arguing against the inclusion of such a clause in its agreement with an airline.

In such an instance, one way of managing such an exposure might be acceptance of the clause with a ceiling or "cap" on the maximum liability. Prudence might also necessitate having proper insurance coverage as a back-up to such a consequential loss indemnity.

It may also consider qualifying or limiting the scope of the consequential loss to the extent that it is covered by insurance:

> *The Contractor shall only be liable for consequential loss or damage to the Principal to the extent that such loss or damage is recoverable by the Contractor (or its sub-contractors and/or agents) under a valid and collectable policy of insurance carried by the Contractor.*

For a more comprehensive discussion on consequential loss, you should consult

Understanding Indemnity Clauses, the first volume in the *Commercial Contracts for Managers Series*.

■■■

Liquidated damages

On occasion, a Principal will require a Contractor to agree to a liquidated damages clause in a contract.

This enables a Principal to place on record a genuine pre-estimate of the amount of damages or loss that it will suffer in the event of a breach by the Contractor. The estimate must be within certain limits and not "out of all proportion".

Liquidated damages can either be a stated dollar amount or an amount easily ascertainable by reference to a fixed scale of charges or by a simple calculation.

It is designed to overcome the necessity for a Principal to otherwise have to prove loss in a claim for damages. By doing so, it can save the Principal time and make the recovery proceedings considerably less expensive for a Principal.

The provision is becoming increasingly common in service contracts.

Penalty

If the agreed figure is not a genuine pre-estimate of the loss, it may be construed by a court to be a penalty. The generally accepted test of whether a liquidated damages claim amounts to a penalty is whether the amount claimed is "extravagant and unconscionable". A court will wish to be satisfied that the amount of liquidated damages specified was calculated as a genuine attempt to pre-assess the likely damages to be involved. The fact that the amount may be merely "unfair" at the time it is enforced may not be sufficient to move a court to strike such a clause down, as the parties will be required to stand by their bargain.

Depending upon the jurisdiction, penalties are generally *void* or *unenforceable* since they are said to be contrary to public policy. As this is a developing area of the law, you should check with your lawyer to establish the correct position for your particular jurisdiction.

Prudent practice (from a Contractor's perspective) requires that some form of *ceiling* or *cap* be placed on any total liquidated damages amount claimed by a Principal.

Ownership of intellectual property

Often, a Contractor will "bring to the table" some form of proprietary information, product or other expertise. Depending upon the circumstances, this can actually be one of the prime reasons behind the Contractor's ultimate selection by the Principal. This category of intellectual property rights may be referred to as *background intellectual property rights.*

Whereas, the intellectual property rights created during the course of a contract are sometimes referred to as *foreground intellectual property rights.*

A Contractor will generally seek to retain *both* categories of rights.

It will depend upon the particular circumstances of the situation whether:

- the Principal is paying the Contractor only for some *limited right to use* such proprietary information; or
- the Principal is paying the Contractor to actually devise or develop such proprietary information for the Principal's exclusive use and ownership.

This is a crucial point to bear in mind. It is something that must be absolutely clear and unequivocal in the contract documentation.

Depending upon the circumstances, the Principal's contract documents may contain provisions either granting the Principal the exclusive ownership of the intellectual property developed by the Contractor or perhaps only granting some form of limited permission for its use. A Principal must be aware that it may be prevented from accessing such intellectual property after termination of the contract. Such an arrangement could effectively tie-up the Principal for many years.

On the other hand, the Principal's failure to have rights over the intellectual property could mean that, if the Contractor defaults, the continued use by the Principal of those intellectual property rights may no longer exist — which could cause the Principal substantial loss and damage.

Moral rights

Note that the concept of *moral rights* exists in some jurisdictions. The moral rights of an author of literary, dramatic, musical or artistic works and cinematograph films are enshrined in legislation in some jurisdictions such as New South Wales. Moral rights generally refers to a right of attribution of authorship or a right of integrity of authorship. For example, if a manuscript is broken up, rearranged and sold in a different form without the author's permission, this may be a breach of the author's moral rights. This applies regardless of whether an author has transferred copyright to another party. Moral rights are non-transferable, which means that they stay with the author always.

Whilst infringement is not an offence under the New South Wales legislation, it does give rise to a right of action by the author or the originator of the work for infringement. Remedies for infringement of moral rights could include:

- the issue of an injunction;
- an award of damages for loss resulting from the infringement;
- a declaration that a moral right has been infringed;
- an order that the defendant make a public apology for the infringement; or
- an order that any false attribution of authorship be removed or reversed.

Your lawyer will be able to best advise you on the necessary safeguards, in the event that your specific situation has the potential to fall into this category.

Third party claims

When dealing with intellectual property issues, it is common (and not unreasonable) for a Principal to seek protection (usually in the form of an indemnity clause) against claims by any third party that:

- the intellectual property claimed to be owned by the Contractor infringes some right of the third party; or
- the use of such intellectual property by the Principal constitutes an infringement of such third party's rights.

In such cases, the Principal is attempting to verify the Contractor's clear ownership and title to the items that the Principal is contracting for the Contractor to supply.

Case study: what's yours is mine

In a situation where a Principal is using the tendering process to gain ideas, it may be tempted to use the process to "borrow" different parts from various tenders to assemble a final product.

A leading property developer **Freefall Developments** (the Principal), conducted a tender for the construction of a large and prestigious urban development called "Pleasant Landings".

Talented and well-known Contractors such as **Perry Shoot** and **Skye Dyver** were anxious to achieve selection for involvement in such a prestigious development. Success in the selection process would provide them with "sky-high" amounts of exposure.

In the bid document, the conditions of tender required prospective Contractors to submit detailed designs for the development, together with their bid document. These designs were conceptualised and prepared at great expense by each of the various Contractors.

Crucially, the conditions of tender provided that the act of submitting the designs to the Principal *transferred the ownership* of them to the Principal, whether the Contractor's bid was successful or otherwise.

This effectively meant that the Principal had many innovative and original designs from which to choose, any and all of which could be effectively had by the Principal free of charge.

In effect, the Principal could have selected one Contractor's design and then chosen another Contractor to implement that design.

Perry Shoot and **Skye Dyver** each viewed their own work as too valuable to simply give away free of charge.

Perry and **Skye**, being prudent Contractors, independently decided to include an intellectual property statement in their respective bid documents, along the following lines:

Intellectual property statement

All concepts, designs, processes, documentation and know-how including but not limited to the process by which same was created, together with the entirety of the service delivery concept, methods and procedures (including all documentation associated therewith) (the "Information") shall at all times be and remain the sole and exclusive intellectual property of the Contractor.

This tender is submitted on the basis that all Information has been acknowledged as confidential to the Contractor and will be kept confidential.

Submission of this bid does not under any circumstances constitute permission or a licence of any kind (express or implied) to use or divulge the Information (or any part thereof) in any way. The use of the Information is expressly limited solely to the evaluation of the tender to assessing the viability of forming a contractual relationship.

In the event that the Contractor's bid is unsuccessful (or if successful, at the conclusion of any contract) all Information in whatever form including any duplicate copies made must either be destroyed (and satisfactory evidence provided of this) or be returned to the Contractor.

Force majeure

A *force majeure* event is an agreed event beyond the control of a party, which frustrates or postpones the ability of that party to perform its obligations under the contract. The key feature of a *force majeure* situation is that the *force majeure* event can be a *temporary* condition delaying performance. Much will, of course, depend on the specific drafting of the *force majeure* clause.

The clause is intended to relieve that party from complying with its obligations under the contract for a certain period (usually, but not always, for the duration of the *force majeure* event).

In most jurisdictions, there is no law defining what actually constitutes a *force majeure* event. Hence, the definition will ultimately depend upon what the parties can agree upon and the way that such agreement is translated into the drafting of the *force majeure* clause.

Definitions will often include things such as "explosion, lightning, quarantine, epidemic, radiation, war, riot, terrorism, insurrection, Act of Parliament, or act of God".

For many prospective Contractors, a hotly debated *force majeure* point is whether to include "strike or industrial dispute" in the definition of a *force majeure* event.

On one side: the Contractor will argue that it will not be able to provide the services if a strike occurs, as it will not have the necessary personnel available.

On the other side: the Principal will argue that it requires and is paying for an uninterrupted service. With this in mind, it is therefore the Contractor's role to manage such risks as part of its business.

It is generally to the benefit of any Contractor supplying goods or services to have such a clause in their contract.

Golden Rule

A prudent Contractor should always consider having a properly drafted *force majeure* clause in any contract, as a safeguard.

■■■

Termination for convenience

The *termination for convenience* clause grants an extremely broad right for a Principal to, unilaterally and without cause, terminate the contract without becoming liable for breach-of-contract damages.

Such clauses are drawn to limit the ability of the party being terminated to recover only *actual costs incurred* plus *profit on work completed.* Such clauses are generally drawn to preclude the recovery of anticipatory profit.

Termination for convenience clauses are not "normal" commercial terms. They are usually found in almost every government contract, however, corporations are increasingly tending to mimic the trend for their use.

The rationale, from a government's perspective, is that long-term contractual arrangements should not constrain a change in government or a change in government policy, that might otherwise cause a waste of taxpayer's money or burden a government with unneeded supplies or outmoded technology.

In general, such clauses operate unilaterally (only one party can terminate the contract for convenience) and therefore do not give the other party the certainty of tenure that a "normal" contract does.

If you must absolutely accept a termination for convenience clause, you should seek to negotiate more favourable terms on reimbursement of the actual costs incurred in demobilisation of any staff, sub-contractors, equipment and materials. For more information on protecting a Contractor's capital investment, see the section on **Capital expenditure** in Chapter 6.

It would also be prudent to negotiate to lengthen the term of notice from the almost ubiquitous 30 days to, say, 90 or even 180 days or an even longer period, depending upon the relevant circumstances.

To reinforce an earlier point made, whatever is said between the parties must be properly recorded and documented. For example, if, during pre-tender negotiations, a Principal states to a Contractor the terms under which a termination for convenience may occur, this may give a right of action by the Contractor against the Principal at a later time, in the event of a dispute.

Time of the essence

Firstly, it is important to understand the meaning of the expression *essential term*. An essential term is a term *fundamental to the basis of the contract itself*; such that if it is not performed, alters the very nature of the contract itself.

In many jurisdictions, an essential term, once breached, gives rise to termination of the contract by the non-defaulting party. The non-defaulting party would then be entitled to sue the defaulting party for any loss suffered in respect of such termination including the concept of loss-of-bargain damages.

The idea of using a *time of the essence* clause, is to make the concept of time (as in the performance of a particular obligation in a contract) an essential term of the contract.

When using time of the essence, *the concept of reasonableness is excluded*. The breach of a time limit by as little as one minute could trigger a breach.

Indeed, the danger of making essential terms of all time stipulations in a contract, is obvious. Every action, under a contract, which is subject to a time limit, becomes an essential term. If such term is breached, it could then give rise to termination of the contract and an action for damages. In any given commercial contract, that could amount to thousands of individual potential instances of risk.

In some jurisdictions, the effect of the time of the essence concept has been called into question and there is no clear determination. However, prudence dictates that you assume the worst and thereby, avoid trouble. Your lawyer can best advise you of the specifics of your jurisdiction and your contractual situation.

■■■

Assignment

An *assignment* (for the purposes of this section) is quite simply a transfer of rights, benefits and obligations under a contract from one party (called the *assignor*) to another party (called the *assignee*).

Principals go to great lengths to select Contractors in a tendering process. They apply a number of criteria to ultimately select the Contractor they believe best fulfils such needs. After such a rigorous process, a Principal will usually wish to ensure that it continues to deal with the entity it had selected. A Principal will usually require the option of terminating the contract in the event of any attempt at substituting the Contractor or in the event of a *change of control* in the Contractor's company (see page 67 for more about **Change of control in the Contractor**). At the very least, a Principal would require some process where it will have the final right of approval of any change in the Contractor.

A Principal, therefore, benefits from having an assignment clause in their contract, restricting and governing the assignment of the Contractor's interest to another party. It will usually contain a restriction preventing any assignment of the Contractor's interest without the Principal's written consent. The primary reason being that another party proposing to take the place of the Contractor will often be unknown to the Principal.

The Principal is entitled to withhold consent to the assignment until:

☑ **certain conditions prescribed by the assignment clause are satisfied by the Contractor;**

For example, the Principal may wish to withhold consent until the existing breaches of the agreement by the Contractor have been remedied.

☑ **the steps prescribed by the assignment clause have been followed by the Contractor (and the incoming party); and**

For example, the Contractor may have to follow certain steps regarding the form and timing of notice to the Principal of the proposed assignment, also regarding the timely provision of relevant information requested by the Principal.

☑ **certain criteria prescribed by the assignment clause have been met by the incoming party.**

For example, the new Contractor may have to establish proof of their reputation, financial strength and stability, a particular type of insurance coverage, trade or bank references, demonstrated skills to be able to perform certain specialised tasks etc. These criteria must be satisfied by the new Contractor to a standard that is no less favourable to the Principal.

A generic assignment clause may look something like this:

ASSIGNMENT

The Contractor shall not assign, mortgage, charge or otherwise deal with or transfer any of its right, title or interest hereunder without the prior written consent of the Principal which consent will not be unreasonably withheld where the Contractor reasonably satisfies the Principal that the proposed assignee is of no less financial strength than the Contractor and is a reputable person or entity that has the capacity, expertise and resources to carry out the obligations under this Agreement.

Change of control in the Contractor

A useful supplement to an assignment clause is the *change of control* clause. This will govern the situation where there is a change in the ownership or control of the Contractor.

For example, a Contractor might be acquired by a company, which the Principal does not consider suitable, or with which the Principal specifically wishes to avoid having any dealings. Another reason might be that the acquiring entity does not have the financial strength and stability required by the Principal. In some cases, the acquiring company may be one of the unsuccessful tenderers.

It is not unheard of for an unsuccessful tenderer to consider acquiring the company selected as the successful tenderer to thereby win the tender "through the back door". This would be especially likely where such a contract carried a considerable financial or strategic significance to the acquirer.

To broaden its scope, the change of control clause will generally also extend to dealing with any change of control over the Contractor's *parent company*.

A further way of broadening the change of control clause is to define one of the events constituting a change of control to be any change in the *effective* control of the company. This caters for situations where an event does not constitute a change in the *legal or ownership* control of the company, but in reality does create a change of *actual* control.

Examples of such an event could be:

- the appointment or removal of all (or the majority) of the directors or other equivalent officers of the Contractor; or
- giving directions with respect to the operating and financial policies of the Contractor, with which the directors or other equivalent officers of the Contractor are obliged to comply.

A change of control clause will generally define the events constituting a change of control. It will generally provide that any change of control (that falls within such definition) will:

- trigger a certain set of events such as termination; or
- may be *deemed* to be an assignment. Such a deeming provision will then trigger the same information and approval processes necessary in an assignment situation.

A generic change of control clause might look something like this:

CHANGE OF CONTROL

(a) ***"Change of Control"*** *for the purposes of this clause means any of the following:*

i. any substantial transfer of share or shares shall be registered, recorded or entered in the books of the Contractor or its ultimate holding company;

ii. any beneficial interest in any of the Contractor's shares shall be dealt with;

iii. any new share in the Contractor shall be issued; or

iv. any other action shall be taken or attempted to be taken,

having the effect that the shareholders of the Contractor or its ultimate holding company at the date hereof together shall beneficially hold or control less than 50% of the voting rights at general meetings of and dividend and capital participation rights of all shareholders in the Contractor or its ultimate holding company, provided that this clause shall not apply where the Contractor or its ultimate holding company is a company of which voting shares are listed on a recognised stock exchange in Australia and the transfer of shares, change in beneficial interest, issue of shares or other such action is a result of normal day to day trading activities for the Contractor's shares or that of its ultimate holding company on the stock exchange.

(b) The Contractor affected by a Change of Control must immediately notify the Principal in writing of that fact and supply all relevant material particulars of the Change of Control to the Principal.

(c) Upon a Change of Control the Principal shall after the date of receipt of notification thereof from the Contractor, be entitled to ...

■■■

Changes to the law

There are obviously competing interests on the issue of changes to the law.

Some contracts will contain provisions dealing with future change in the law or other administrative regulations, which could affect the parties, services or price.

For example, the introduction of a new tax on the goods or services being provided by the Contractor immediately triggers the question: *Who will bear this new cost?* Remember that it will be a cost or other impediment not previously contemplated by the parties when the contract was negotiated and entered into.

A prudent Contractor will wish to include a clause dealing with the issue to avoid any doubt that the Principal will bear the risk of changes to the law.

With an appropriately drafted clause, the introduction of a new tax would enable the Contractor to pass on the effect of the new tax to the Principal, thereby preserving the Contractor's margins and profitability.

Case study: Is our contract future-proof?

How not to use a "future changes to the law" provision to outsmart yourself

A contract for the provision of certain goods and services by **Denver Contracting** ("**Denver**") to the Principal, **Aspen Group** ("**Aspen**") contained the following clause:

> *In the event of the introduction of any new tax, excise, levy or impost or of the increase in any existing taxes, excises, levies or imposts upon receiving notice from the Contractor, the Principal shall enter into negotiations with the Contractor to renegotiate the Contract Pricing.*

In the event of a failure to reach agreement, the contract provided that if the dispute was "genuine" and concerning "a fundamental issue", that either party could terminate the agreement.

The contract was a five-year agreement and the contract pricing was increased on a yearly basis pursuant to a detailed and complex formula contained within the agreement.

In the second year of the contract, the government introduced a doubling of the existing goods and services tax.

At that time, there was a severe economic downturn in the sector within which **Denver** operated. Many competitors were idle and looking to take on work wherever they could.

With the increase in the tax, there was little doubt that **Denver's** margins were going to suffer. The CEO of **Denver**, **Col O'Rado** thought he could present a good case for a justified price increase to **Aspen**. **Denver** formally gave notice to **Aspen** requiring the contract pricing to be renegotiated.

Aspen capitalised on this turn of events by subtly insinuating that a competitor of **Denver**, called **Canyon Contracting**, was prepared to take on this contract for 20% per annum less than **Denver** was currently charging **Aspen**.

Denver realised that it had triggered an event over which it had lost control and ultimately backfired. To retain the contract, **Denver** was forced to accept a 20% price decrease.

> As **Denver** learned to its great detriment, great care must be exercised in drafting contract clauses dealing with changes in the law — to avoid triggering a general renegotiation on price.
>
> As occurred in **Denver's** case, other factors totally unrelated to the new tax (such as a competitor's price, increased volumes or depressed market conditions) became relevant. These other factors were then used, to great effect, by the Principal to obtain an actual net price reduction.
>
> The provision, ideally, should have simply automatically passed-on the net increase in prices to the Principal. Or, at the very least, any new negotiations should have been restricted to *taking into account the impact of such new tax, excise, levy or impost.*

■■■

Governing law and jurisdiction

Parties need to agree upon the applicable law governing the contract document, in the event of any dispute or call for interpretation of the contents of the document.

The contract should specify the particular state or country under which the contract will be governed and interpreted. For example, such a statement will specifically declare the contract to be governed by and interpreted under the laws of New South Wales, the laws of England, the State of California USA, etc.

This is usually accompanied by a statement of the jurisdiction or *forum* (place) for the settlement of any disputes arising.

Usually, the Principal (wisely) chooses its own local jurisdiction.

A form of the jurisdiction clause, may look similar to the following:

> *This Agreement shall be governed by and construed in accordance with the laws of New South Wales, Australia. Each party irrevocably and unconditionally:*
>
> ***a)*** *submits to the [exclusive or non-exclusive] jurisdiction of the courts of New South Wales; and*
>
> ***b)*** *waives any and all claims or objections based on absence of jurisdiction or inconvenient forum.*

For a more detailed examination of jurisdiction clauses and an explanation of the differences between exclusive and non-exclusive jurisdiction, you should consult ***Understanding Commonly Used Contract Terms: Boilerplate Clauses***, the fourth volume in the *Commercial Contracts for Managers Series.*

Chapter 5

ASPECTS OF CONTRACT EVALUATION

Contract management, in the context used in this book, concerns the management of the large volume of contract documents encountered by many organisations.

It is important to note that the issue is not necessarily confined to companies engaged in tendering but extends to any company that enters into contracts on a regular basis.

The primary issue covered in this chapter relates to the method of contract evaluation in a tendering situation. This is potentially one of the areas of the greatest risk of exposure to liability for many Contractors.

It is all very well to understand commercial contracts, however, if there is no method or system in place dealing with the way contracts are scrutinised, very few contracts will ever be subjected to review. Consequently, very little of the knowledge acquired from the *Commercial Contracts for Managers Series*, can ever be applied.

Given the large number of contracts and tenders that most organisations deal with on a daily basis, it is important to ensure that sufficient controls and safeguards exist, to adequately manage the legal risk or exposure underlying each of the contracts entered into by the organisation.

Businesses typically deal with more contracts each year. The combination of both the size and complexity of those contracts and (more often than not) the extremely tight deadlines faced, create a problem.

The problem tends to manifest itself in situations where a company is frequently engaged in tendering processes to win work.

Generally, two major steps need to be taken to confront this problem. Prudent organisations will:

1) devise and produce a contracts' management policy; and

2) standardise the forms of contract for each business unit throughout the organisation.

Consequences of inadequate systems

Because of the lack of time available, and the scarcity of human resources, contracts may sometimes be entered into that do not fully protect the interests of a tenderer. As a result, companies selling their goods and/or services, may find themselves bound to unreasonably harsh terms in a contract, ultimately eroding their forecasted profitability.

In some instances, harsh contract terms can even cause large losses on a contract. For example, giving blanket indemnities beyond what should reasonably be covered, such as the instance where a Contractor indemnifies the other party for the negligence of that other party.

Another instance might be where a Contractor finds itself in a situation where its prices are fixed for an inordinately long period of time. Where its initial estimates proved to be incorrect or optimistic, the Contractor winds up in a loss-making situation, from which there is no escape.

Implementing systems

In many businesses, adequate contract evaluation controls need to be considered. In devising such controls and procedures, they must be of a sufficient standard to be:

- practically workable and adding real value to business processes;
- easy to follow;
- clear and unequivocal; and
- enforced to ensure universal adoption throughout the business.

It is important to ensure that any improvements instituted be organically able to cope with future acquisitions and proposed growth.

It is of questionable benefit to put into place an ad-hoc infrastructure that will be rendered obsolete as soon as there is another acquisition or phase of growth. A system that needs to be constantly reinvented every year or two creates more problems than it solves.

The primary issue that must be dealt with by any Contractor is:

What method should be utilised to assess and evaluate client tenders and incoming contract documents?

■■■

Inherent conflict of interest

There is an inherent conflict of interest in the way that many organisations scrutinise and evaluate incoming contracts (that is, contracts submitted to the organisation by another party).

They may either:

- allow the *operations* part of the business to carry out such a task. The rationale being that they are the persons that will end up actually providing the goods and/or services that are the subject of the contract. Therefore, they will be best placed to know whether they will be able to work to the contract; or
- entrust the process of incoming contract evaluation to their *business development* staff (sales persons). The rationale for this is that they are the "prospectors" for the organisation and have a broad knowledge of the organisation's systems and capabilities.

Certainly, the input of both sales and operations people is always useful and valuable in relation to assessing the viability of commercial aspects of a deal. There is always a place for their input and viewpoint to provide a practical and "real-world" perspective to any contract review.

Their value, however, will not usually extend to providing a proper assessment of the *legal* aspects and risks of a particular transaction.

The primary reason is that salespeople are driven by other priorities and motivations. The zeal to close a deal may, in some instances, compromise the judgment of that salesperson into accepting unduly onerous terms.

Often, the rewards of salespersons are based on the number of deals and/or the volume of business brought into the organisation. The organisation's compliance with the terms of contract then becomes someone else's problem. Therefore, allowing commission-based salespeople to be the sole evaluators of incoming contracts, could be said by some, to be akin to allowing the proverbial fox to guard the chickens.

Sometimes, operations personnel may (with the best of intentions) be tempted to think that they can overcome a badly-worded contract document, by good management and impeccable customer-service. Unfortunately, the reality is that relationships cannot always overcome bad contract terms.

The only way to maintain control over the outcome of the contract review process is to have a policy in place at the *front end* of the process and to rigidly enforce it.

■■■

Decentralising contract evaluations

In a decentralised model, contract evaluations are performed within the subsidiary or business unit that will actually perform the obligations under the contract.

The inherent danger of decentralising the evaluation of contracts is the establishment of inadequate parameters. Sufficient parameters are difficult to define and require constant monitoring to ensure they are being complied with.

An example of a parameter might relate to the dollar value of a contract.

Head office approval is required for any contract with a revenue exceeding $X per annum.

However, measuring contractual risk by dollar value alone is not always wise. You may recall an example appearing in ***Understanding Indemnity Clauses*** (the first volume in the *Commercial Contracts for Managers Series*) that related to a $60 per month agreement to licence a car-parking space. The acceptance of an indemnity clause (which included coverage for the other party's negligence), created a situation of almost unlimited potential liability. The important principle that emerged was that the size or "dollar value" of a contract alone does not limit the amount of potential liability under the contract.

It is unrealistic to expect non-legal personnel to assume the mantle of a lawyer by arming them with a simple "how-to" manual and some brief instruction. It is unfair to expect these people to make a correct "borderline" call or sometimes to even recognise that a case may be more complex than it appears to be.

The extent of the monitoring required (of the personnel charged with the task of contract evaluation staff, together with random checks on particular contracts) can lead to a wasteful duplication of efforts, in laboriously re-checking contracts after the event.

In a decentralised model, there is a risk that the role of senior management is reduced to policing and monitoring *after the event.* Often, by the time an act of non-compliance is discovered, the organisation may be committed to it and it could be too late to avert the relevant consequences.

Organisations need to move away from a defensive and *reactive* role of catching people out "doing the wrong thing". A more *proactive* stance is an ideal way of leading an organisation toward compliance.

Unfortunately, many organisations, while unwilling to spend money on prevention, willingly spend large amounts of time and money fixing a problem that has manifested itself, because of the immediacy and necessity of achieving a solution. This is because such spending will produce a tangible result.

Front-end preventative measures do not have the direct *appearance* of generating any demonstrable savings on the bottom line at the end of each month. However, such preventative measures work best when they are seamless and inconspicuous.

Rectifying problems at the "back-end" (after the worst has happened) is always more costly and disruptive to an organisation. The cost goes beyond the dollar value of the "fix" alone. There is the loss of productivity, the potential loss of reputation etc.

Organisations that can benefit from decentralising are those of a certain size that might have a lawyer within a business unit — who can understand and apply the criteria and parameters which are of material significance to the head office — in order to more effectively manage the review of contracts.

Contract management policy

A well-constructed contract management policy should effectively deal with the following issues:

- levels of contract review and signoff based on the level of risk associated with a contract. Remember, that basing a risk assessment of a contract on dollar value alone is dangerous;
- tender bidding procedures;
- introduction and use of standard forms of contract;
- document execution procedures;
- document security;
- document retention;
- document destruction; and
- a manual *and* education programme covering all of the above.

For a more detailed treatment of contract evaluation and management, you should consult ***Understanding Effective Contract Evaluation***, the sixth volume in the *Commercial Contracts for Managers Series*.

Chapter 6

OTHER ISSUES IN TENDERING

■■■

Relationship between tenderer and Principal — partnerships or "pistols at dawn"?

As always, in the bid documents, a tenderer has a tendency to be in "sales mode" in its attempts to impress the Principal to be selected.

On the other hand, the Principal is trying to maximise the benefits to itself of having a competitive process, hoping that the tenderers will "pull out all stops" to try and outdo one another.

When in sales mode, a Contractor will do all that it can to make the Principal feel good and secure about selecting the Contractor for the job.

One method currently in vogue is the idea that the Contractor and the Principal will work together in a *partnership* to achieve the Principal's goals.

This expression may be fine in conversational terms, however, at law, partnerships carry with them an altogether different significance.

At law, a partnership carries some onerous obligations. The most significant is the ability of *one* partner to make a commitment or enter into an undertaking that *jointly and severally* binds the other partner/s (even without the knowledge of the other partner/s).

Clearly, this is not the intent of two parties on "opposing" sides contracting at arm's-length.

Non-binding statement of partnership

One should also exercise caution with some forms of the "non-binding statement of partnership". This has become an increasingly common feature of some service contracts, in tendering situations. For example, some of these consist of flowery statements of how the parties will continue to co-operate and "love" one another. Then comes "the crunch" when the statement is expressed to be binding upon the Contractor, but *non-binding* upon the Principal.

Therefore, when a Contractor attempts to exercise or enforce any rights against the Principal, the "shield" of "partnership" is raised against the Contractor. A Contractor attempting to assert rights against a Principal by the use of litigation will, no doubt, be met by a Principal's claims that an approach using any kind of "force" is inconsistent with the notion that the parties are partners working co-operatively together.

However, if the Principal has occasion to exercise any right against the Contractor, it can cheerfully proceed to do so with impunity and without remorse. Such a "partnership" obligation applies only unilaterally upon the Contractor.

The enforceability and real effect of such a "partnership" statement may be questionable in some jurisdictions.

Golden Rule

Beware of the "non-binding statement of partnership".

If confronted by one, be sure to carefully read and fully understand the implications of any such statement before accepting and signing it.

Capital expenditure (CAPEX)

Certain types of contracts will require a certain investment of capital by a Contractor.

CAPEX is defined as any expenditure that will appear as a *non current asset* in the Contractor's own financial accounts. For example, a catering company's expenditure on purchases of linen and cutlery in a major five-year catering contract would be classified as a non current asset and any replacements within that time due to either wear and tear or loss (shrinkage), would be classified as expenses.

In some circumstances, an innovative approach by a Contractor, in this area, may attract a sympathetic and favourable viewing by the Principal.

Before submitting a CAPEX proposal in a tender, most Contractors will have a number of organisational thresholds to meet and a certain defined processes to follow internally.

For example, in the case of larger organisations, there will be specific limits of expenditure that can be approved at a local level, without requiring regional or even head office approval.

Many organisations will also have specific *return on capital employed* (ROCE) requirements that must be met to gain internal organisational approval for CAPEX authorisation. ROCE is generally calculated by reference to the following formula:

$$\frac{\textbf{Operating Profit}}{\textbf{(Fixed Assets + Working Capital)}}$$

The above formula is generally computed on a 12-month rolling average, to avoid any short-term distortions.

In many organisations, a business case for CAPEX approval is usually required (among other things) to demonstrate an expected ROCE of somewhere around 15%-20% (this can be dependent upon the individual corporate benchmarks as well as the industry itself).

For a larger organisation, such as a multi-national, a commercially viable *internal rate of return* (IRR) would rarely be expected to be below 10% — especially since in many organisations the average cost of capital may itself be in the vicinity of 10%.

Golden nugget

A word about working capital

When a business makes an investment decision, it must not only consider the financial outlay involved in any CAPEX, but must also take account of the additional burden on working capital that any expansion of activity brings.

Increasing sales tend to require an increase in inventories and consequent increases in the level of debtors. A general increase in the business' scale of operations tends to require the need for greater levels of cash.

To combat the increasing costs of keeping higher levels of inventory, greater efficiency in inventory handling and logistics are required. This means that every item of inventory and every order the organisation receives needs to move at a greater speed (to be converted into cash), thereby lowering the business' working capital requirements.

There is a trend toward stricter working capital management in many organisations. By accelerating and more closely monitoring receivables, payables and inventories, a business may avail itself of a convenient (and often "hidden") source of cash, rather than relying more heavily on external (and more expensive) sources of funding such as banks or equity markets.

From a Principal's perspective, it will typically wish to see a Contractor commit itself to the highest amount of CAPEX possible for two reasons:

1) this will demonstrate the Contractor's level of commitment to the Principal; and

2) whatever amount the Contractor allocates will be money that the Principal itself will not be required to outlay directly.

While most Contractors are happy to spend money to make money (within reasonable limits), they will want to see their investment protected, especially in the event of an early termination of the contract.

A Contractor will generally seek to amortise its CAPEX investment over the term of the contract. However, where the contract term is either relatively short or where the investment is a particularly large one in durable goods such as plant, machinery and motor vehicles, this may not always be possible. In such an event, a mechanism will need to be put into place providing for the Principal to buy-back the equipment at the end of the term or upon earlier termination (see **Termination for convenience**, page 61).

It is important to realise that a Principal will usually not wish to carry any such expenditure of capital on its balance sheet. It is happier carrying the cost indirectly as a profit-and-loss item billed to it by the Contractor. With this in mind, it is generally easier to convince a Principal to agree to a clause providing for the Contractor's ultimate replacement to be compelled to buy-back the CAPEX goods at an agreed value or their then-current book-value.

■■■

Pricing

A Contractor will normally do all things possible to ensure that the contract pricing is not fixed for the entire term of the contract (unless there are valid reasons for actually doing this), without an appropriate allowance for "rise and fall".

Ideally, a prudent Contractor should ensure that it has the ability to review pricing on a periodic basis, say annually.

The costs of materials may fluctuate during the currency of the contract. To reflect this, a Contractor will seek that an appropriate allowance be made in the contract for such "rise and fall". Rise and fall clauses in contracts are also used to adjust the wage component of contract costs in line with movements in the cost of labour.

On occasion, a contract may provide for a periodic price review to be determined "by agreement" of the parties. Where the parties are deadlocked on the issue or fall into dispute because the Principal does not agree to the Contractor's proposals for pricing review, the ideal contractual position for a Contractor is to be able to terminate the contract without penalty and "walk away". Obviously, such a proposal would meet with some degree of resistance from a Principal, who would far prefer that a dispute resolution mechanism be triggered, rather than an automatic termination of the contract.

The pricing of *variations* to the scope of works is also an important consideration. We will talk more about this in the next section on **Variations to the scope of works**.

Also, the Contractor should ensure that there is sufficient provision in the contract enabling it to pass onto the Principal any goods and services tax, *as well as* making allowance for any other taxes or levies that may be imposed in the future. (See also **Changes to the law**, page 70.)

Golden Rule

It is always good practice for a Contractor to make proper allowances for "rise and fall" in its pricing.

Variation to the scope of works

Consider the following clause:

> *The Contractor will not require a variation in the contract fees where the Principal requires a variation of the services which is not substantial.*

If the parties dispute what is "substantial", then it will be necessary for the matter to be resolved under the dispute resolution provisions of the Contract.

It must be understood that the term "substantial" will mean different things to different people. A "substantial" amount of money to someone poor might be $1000. Whereas, a billionaire might regard a much higher amount as being "substantial".

In the same way, a reference to a "substantial price increase" in a contract would carry a different meaning for a large multinational corporation than it would for a small privately held company.

Words such as "substantial" cannot be used as objective measures or reference points. They are not conducive to certainty. A common theme you will find recurring in the *Commercial Contract for Managers Series* is the following:

> ***Uncertainty is the enemy of the businessperson.***

> ***Golden Rule***
>
> Uncertainty encourages litigation.
>
> You should, therefore, avoid vague, uncertain and ambiguous words in contracts.

A prudent Contractor will ensure that a contract contains clear provisions concerning:

- requests by a Principal for variations — procedure should be followed and clear limits on variations should be set; and
- a defined mechanism for the pricing of any such variations.

A preferred Contractor's solution is a variations procedure that would allow the Contractor to submit a quote on a Principal's request for variations. The Principal would then be free to either accept or reject such quotation.

However, such a scenario is comparatively rare in most agreements, as most Principals would not wish to then have to embark on a new search for an outside Contractor to perform the variation works. Most tender specifications will make it clear that the preferred tenderer will be required to cater for all of the Principal's requirements within a given field of endeavour.

Disputes

Once signed, contract documents tend only to be referred to when the parties are in dispute and relationships between parties deteriorate. By the time the "gloves come off", the lines of communication become severely strained or even severed. By this stage, logic and reason are not at their peak.

Once the parties consult their lawyers, there is a risk that the advice they receive will be restricted to the wording of the contract document, sometimes in isolation of the background and context of the dispute.

Disputes can end up following one of three possible paths (in order of escalating magnitude, cost, aggravation and damage to commercial relationships):

1) they are resolved between the parties, without external assistance;
2) they proceed to some form of alternative dispute resolution (ADR) method;
3) they proceed to litigation.

Each of the three methods above will produce a result. However, the consequences and eventual "fallout" will differ considerably between the three methods.

The first method, resolution between the parties is obviously the preferred one in terms of low-cost, low aggravation and maintenance of relationships. The parties have a much better chance of being able to continue to work together in harmony after the dispute is resolved.

The second method, ADR has gained much favour with organisations in recent times. This is because it often represents the best compromise between the three methods available. In theory it retains most of the benefits of the first method, whilst eliminating most of the disadvantages of litigation.

The third method, litigation differs from the first two methods in that a solution is ultimately *imposed* upon the parties. Also, the disadvantages of higher costs and drain on management time are significant factors. Furthermore, the element of confidentiality is lost. The dispute and all the evidence presented becomes a matter of public record. Press headlines concerning litigation ultimately do no favours for either litigant, even for the winner. This is because the focus will tend be on highlighting the shortcomings of both parties. Rarely is one party completely and totally "in the right" and blameless. There generally tends to be "dirty laundry" on both sides. The "dirty laundry" of one party will almost certainly receive an airing by the opposing party (sometimes — but not always — the best form of defence is attack).

The timeframes of litigation are measured in years. The costs can be horrendous, sometimes even out of proportion to the scale of the original dispute. The parties are rarely able to continue working together after litigation. For these reasons, litigation is, and should always be, the method of last recourse in a commercial situation.

For more detailed information about litigation and dispute resolution you should consult ***Understanding Commercial Litigation***, the seventh volume in the *Commercial Contracts for Managers Series.*

■■■

Alternative dispute resolution (ADR)

Methods other than traditional litigation in courts are becoming increasingly popular, particularly as they can provide solutions more quickly and at lower costs.

ADR methods tend to have the benefits of confidentiality and informality. Everything that is said or disclosed is not a matter of public record as it would be in most traditional courts.

Also the savings in legal costs can be considerable. However, such cost savings can be negated in the instance where an arbitration hearing is appealed by referring the matter to a court for a rehearing before a judge.

Also, on the question of costs, one must remember that expenses such as:

- the hiring of rooms;
- stenographers and/or recording equipment (to create a transcript of the proceedings);
- the Arbitrator/s' fees;

must be paid by the participants. The cost savings can sometimes be less than first thought.

One of the primary benefits of ADR is speed. This is often a significant point to be considered, especially in relation to a long term contract, where the outcome can affect the parties significantly in the future.

The most often-used methods of ADR in escalating order are:

1) Good faith negotiations between the chief executive officers of each party and (in some circumstances) a lawyer.

2) Mediation, which is becoming a more popular method. This involves the use of an independent and impartial mediator whose role is to encourage the parties to find positive ways of resolving their differences in an amicable and non-confrontational way. The mediator does not provide a binding decision at the end of the mediation but if the final settlement terms are acceptable, the parties can agree to be bound by them.

3) Arbitration is almost akin to a private and slightly less formal trial. Procedure and rules of evidence are generally adhered to in arbitration proceedings. An arbitrator is appointed who (similarly to a judge in a court) hears the evidence, rules on objections during the hearing and will make findings of fact and issue a decision on the dispute. Depending upon the jurisdiction, there may be:

    - a right to have the matter reheard in court;
    - a limited right of appeal to a court; or
    - a prohibition on any appeal or rehearing of the matter in a court.

Parties can agree to use any one of these methods to deal with a dispute, or a combination of methods. For example, before resorting to litigation, a contract might provide that the parties first enter into negotiations between the chief executive officers of the respective parties. If that proves unsuccessful, the next step may generally be to have the matter mediated and so on.

There may be a provision in a contract preventing recourse to a court before exhausting all of the prescribed ADR remedies. A wise qualification to make to such a clause is an exception for "urgent interlocutory applications".

One of the difficulties with ADR is that the methods may not always be as final and conclusive as they are in traditional courts. It is important to also be aware that an arbitration award obtained in one jurisdiction may not be enforceable in certain other jurisdictions. This consideration is particularly relevant where the other party is a foreign entity.

The use of ADR methods can be provided for in a contract by including an appropriate ADR clause. Dispute resolution clauses generally require use of ADR as either a precursor or alternative to arbitration or litigation. In a number of countries, there are various dispute resolution centres or agencies that are able to provide commercial mediators. These organisations often provide their own preferred boilerplate mediation and ADR clauses.

You should ensure that you seek advice from a qualified lawyer in the appropriate jurisdiction/s applicable to your contract, before consenting to the inclusion of ADR clauses in a contract, particularly where such clauses attempt to usurp or otherwise oust the jurisdiction of the courts.

Golden Rule

Place strict time limits on ADR procedures, especially where court proceedings must be deferred until after the prescribed ADR avenues have been exhausted.

The absence of time limits could prolong "good faith negotiations between the parties" indefinitely.

Obligation to act reasonably

In the United States of America, it is common for contracts to expressly impose an obligation of good faith and fair dealing upon the parties to that contract.

In the absence of a special relationship — such as that of employer–employee or insurer–insured — in most jurisdictions, there appears to be no general obligation in contract law for arm's-length commercial parties to a contract, to act reasonably. In some jurisdictions, however, this duty may be implied.

The question remains, what does it mean to act "reasonably"?

A typical lawyer's answer would be that it depends on the circumstances. A cynic might suggest it is "whatever you can get away with" without breaching a contract or being accused of being fraudulent.

In many contracts, especially government contracts, the contract administrator (a delegate representing the Principal) has very wide and extensive powers. On occasion, the personality of the contract administrator can have a substantial effect on the working relationship with the Contractor and in extreme cases, perhaps also on the Contractor's profitability.

To overcome any doubts, the inclusion into a contract of a clause similar to the following, can be a useful tool:

> *Wherever the Principal or Contract Administrator is required to make any decision or determination, give any direction, exercise any discretion, form any opinion, give any interpretation or exercise any powers, it shall at all times act reasonably and do so upon reasonable grounds.*

Case study:

Be reasonable! The power of a contract administrator

Blackboard Enterprises (**"Blackboard"**) was selected as the successful tenderer for an extremely lucrative and sought-after contract with the (fictitious) **Department of Schooling and Learning**, to perform building maintenance at all of its educational facilities (numbering in the thousands) throughout the country.

The tendering process was a highly competitive, extremely expensive and time-consuming one.

Fortunately for **Blackboard**, the **Department of Schooling and Learning** had allowed **Blackboard** time to negotiate a number of contractual issues after the selection process for the successful tenderer was complete.

One of the terms of the contract provided that:

> ***Blackboard*** *shall obey all directions of the Contract Administrator.*

Under the contract, the **Department of Schooling and Learning** was permitted to appoint a contract administrator. The contract administrator was effectively the Department's delegate — permitted to exercise all of the contractual powers invested in the Department.

Note there was no element of "reasonableness" contained anywhere within the contract, concerning the contract administrator's exercise of any discretion, the making of any decision, the giving of any direction or other use of its powers.

Another provision in the contract was an indemnity clause providing that:

> ***Blackboard*** *indemnifies and holds harmless the* ***Department of Schooling and Learning*** *and its officers, employees, Authorised Delegates, and contractors against any loss, damage, injury, death or any cost or expense caused by the actions of* ***Blackboard****.*

Note that the indemnity contains no qualifications, for example, restricting liability only to **Blackboard's** *negligent* acts.

The Department's appointed contract administrator, **Hugh Teechum**, was a notoriously cantankerous individual with a reputation for being difficult.

Blackboard's legal counsel wisely considered a situation where the contract administrator, **Hugh**, were to direct that **Blackboard** demolish a particular structure. **Blackboard** would, of course, be obliged to obey the direction given by **Hugh**, or otherwise risk breaching the contract and risk possible termination consequences.

However, an incongruous situation could conceivably arise where the **Department of Schooling and Learning** could then make a claim against **Blackboard** — under the indemnity clause — for the loss of the structure that **Blackboard** had demolished. **Blackboard** would then be liable to the **Department** for the demolished structure, notwithstanding the fact that **Blackboard** was acting on a direction from **Hugh** to do so.

Whilst the situation sounds bizarre, such potential uncertainties in a contract can (at best) potentially damage hard-won relationships and (at worst) lead to litigation.

Fortunately, a workable solution was found to the problem by the agreement of both parties to amend the two clauses referred to above to read as follows. Added text is <u>underlined</u> and deleted text is shown as ~~strikethrough~~.

> *The Contractor* ***(Blackboard)*** *shall obey all reasonable and lawful directions of the Contract Administrator* ***(Hugh)*** *that are necessary for the proper administration of the Contract provided that such directions do not place the Contractor in a position of breaching the Contract.*
>
> and
>
> *The Contractor* ***(Blackboard)*** *indemnifies and holds harmless the* ***Department of Schooling and Learning*** *and its officers, employees, Authorised Delegates, and contractors against any loss, damage, injury, death or any cost or expense caused by the ~~actions~~ act, omission or negligence of the Contractor* ***(Blackboard)*** *and only to the extent so caused. This shall not extend to include any consequential loss, damage, injury or death.*
>
> In this situation, an "obligation to act reasonably" clause (similar to that described earlier) would also be an advisable inclusion, from the Contractor's perspective.

A Principal may have some concerns about accepting such a clause as it may be required to prove (sometimes with difficulty) that it has been "reasonable".

Most courts are not prepared to imply an obligation on a Principal to act reasonably in the exercise of any powers under the contract. In jurisdictions where the duty is not implied, a court will consider that such a duty is not necessary for the proper commercial operation of the contract. Your lawyer should be consulted to establish the exact position in your jurisdiction.

Golden Rule

If you expect or require the other party to the contract to have to act reasonably in its dealings with you, you should explicitly state this in the contract.

Sub-contracts

Often, a Contractor must rely upon specialised sub-contractors to assist it in providing goods or services to a Principal.

In such an event, a prime issue of importance for a Contractor is to have an appropriate "back-to-back" contract with such sub-contractor. "Back-to-back" in this instance simply means that the obligations contained in the Contractor's agreement with the Principal (the *head-contract*), that are applicable to the sub-contractor, are accurately and directly mirrored in the agreement with the sub-contractor (the *sub-contract*).

Otherwise, if a Contractor uses a form of contract different to the head-contract (or sometimes no written contract!), there is a very real risk that some obligations under the head-contract may be missed.

The "gap" thereby created will *always* be the responsibility of the Contractor. Such a "gap" could have a significant cost impact and in some cases could turn an otherwise profitable contract into a loss-making one for the Contractor.

This is because the Contractor carries primary responsibility to the Principal under the head-contract. In fact, some head-contracts will make specific provision (though it is arguably not necessary to do so) that in the event that a Contractor sub-contracts services, it will always be primarily liable to the Principal if anything goes wrong.

This is because a Principal will not want to have to exercise its rights under the head-contract with parties other than the one it has contracted with; that is, the Contractor.

In the event that a Contractor becomes liable to a Principal for any wrongdoing of a sub-contractor, the Contractor may certainly have pursuable rights against that sub-contractor. However, this simply adds to the Contractor's pain as it ends up having two battles to fight; one with the Principal and one with the sub-contractor. The Contractor's legal costs increase as a result, and matters can become downright messy.

The situation is considerably worsened, from a Contractor's perspective, in the event that the sub-contractor had no assets against which to make any recovery or went out of business or into liquidation.

The best that a Contractor can do to shield itself against this type of situation (other than exercising the utmost care in the selection of reputable sub-contractors) is to:

- have a proper back-to-back agreement with all sub-contractors to seal off any "gaps"; and
- ensure that all sub-contractors have an adequate and continuing insurance policy — against which recourse can be had by the Contractor in the event of the worst occurring.

For certain services, professional indemnity insurance for sub-contractors is a necessity. Otherwise, a Contractor should require a sub-contractor to, at least, have in place a policy covering it for any errors and omissions.

■■■

Collusive tendering and other questionable practices

It is perhaps helpful, at this point, to restate one of the initial points made earlier; the rationale motivating a Principal to establish a tendering process is to *generate sufficient competitive forces* to:

- obtain the best price/quality mix;
- obtain the best value for money;
- provide the best and most efficient solution; and
- ensure probity, fairness and transparency in the selection process.

Collusive tendering and other questionable practices in fact go some way towards nullifying those very benefits. The objective of getting the work done at the lowest possible cost but receiving the best quality is never achieved.

Collusive tendering occurs where two or more (or sometimes even all) Contractors collude by submitting what appear to be independent tender bids. The collusive bidders have an understanding between themselves that the successful bidder will either pay certain sums to the unsuccessful members of the colluding group or will engage them to perform significant parts of the work as sub-contractors, often at higher than usual margins.

The benefits to the colluding group are:

- they share contracts by rotation with substantial profit margins virtually assured, as their bids collectively keep the costs artificially high;
- they all share in the profits from works carried out by other members of the colluding group.

Other collusive tendering practices may include any of the following scenarios:

- any discussion between tenderers (in the absence of the Principal) of their respective tenders prior to their submission, which might result in or produce any disadvantage to the Principal;
- any other exchange of information between tenderers not disclosed to the Principal, prior to the award of the contract; and
- an agreement between tenderers to fix prices or other any conditions of contract.

Other questionable practices may include:

- submission of a tender without a firm intention to proceed with the work (this might be done to advantage another tenderer or disadvantage the Principal);
- the existence of an undeclared conflict of interest; or
- the payment of any secret commission.

In government tendering, there has been an increasing recognition of the existence of these practices. Hence, the current use of "certificates of compliance" or "certificates of collusive tendering" or "probity declarations".

These documents usually take the form of a statutory declaration made by the managing director of the organisation submitting the bid. The declaration attests to the fact that the bid is "clean" (ie, has not been arrived at by collusive or other questionable or unethical means).

An example of such a declaration can be seen in Appendix E.

Chapter 7

CONCLUSION

The use of tendering as a contract-letting tool was traditionally the province of the public sector for government contracts. However, in recent times, the private sector has made use of tendering as a competitive bargaining tool with the multitude of Contractors seeking to win more business.

As a result of Principals becoming more sophisticated and accustomed to using the method, many Contractors report that tendering has become a much more intensive and difficult process.

Checklist: why tenders are becoming more demanding

- ☑ Organisations are more sophisticated consumers of goods and services and hence, have clearer ideas of their requirements.
- ☑ Markets are becoming more transparent and accessible.
- ☑ The lowest price is not necessarily the primary consideration.

Checklist: why tenders are becoming more demanding — *continued*

- ☑ Optimising the price/quality mix is becoming of greater importance.
- ☑ Cultural compatibility of organisations is of growing importance.
- ☑ Beyond the Contractor's organisation itself, of increasing significance are the skills, qualifications and other characteristics possessed by individuals within the organisation, involved in the delivery of the goods and/or services.
- ☑ Greater emphasis is being placed upon a Contractor coming up with innovative ways of providing the goods and delivering the services.
- ☑ The requirements to adhere to and implement policies recognising input from minority and other special interest groups are becoming more stringent.
- ☑ There is a trend to outsourcing more areas of risk to the Contractor.
- ☑ There is greater pressure to deliver complementary and value-added services, such as training.

Where a Principal negotiates a one-sided agreement unfairly biased against the Contractor, this can often be a tremendous incentive for the Contractor, during the life of the contract, to cut corners in service delivery, be tempted to use inferior materials or otherwise continually raise objections or seek variations. This can make the initial "win" by the Principal a hollow victory indeed.

By now, you should have gained an appreciation of the typical steps through which a tenderer must proceed in order to make a proper assessment of whether to bid and if so, on what terms.

Also, an understanding of the selection criteria used by a Principal is a vital step in helping an organisation formulate its tender proposal, to specifically address such criteria in the best manner possible.

A number of the difficulties and potential pitfalls that can befall the prospective tenderer have been made apparent, as well as ideas on appropriate ways of overcoming them. You will also have gained insights from both the perspective of Principal and Contractor on various issues of significance that commonly arise in a Principal/Contractor relationship.

It should now be a little easier to be able to detect the absence of essential clauses in a contract attached to a tender bundle, and to know what is required to obtain some basic safeguards. You should also be better able to ascertain when another party is being overzealous or overstepping the bounds of reasonableness in their drafting of such a document.

The intricate relationship between contract evaluation and the tendering process should also be apparent.

Ideally, you have gained an appreciation of the relevant steps required to critically evaluate and scrutinise a tender bundle (with your organisation's capabilities in mind) prior to accepting it. You will also be in a better position to gain the most benefit from your lawyer and bid team when working with them on your next tender.

By this time, any reader should also be "sold" on the merits of having systems and processes in place for both tendering and contract evaluation. Such systems and processes — particularly in larger Contractor organisations — can help eliminate the personality influences that can sometimes lead to unnecessary departures from company policies and quality assurance procedures. If allowed to occur, such unauthorised departures would tend to detract from the professional image of the Contractor organisation.

Such systems and processes also help in "smoothing-over" the wide variance in competency levels inherent in any large organisation, that might otherwise tend to undermine organisational consistency.

Note about the Appendices:

- The documents shown are intended purely as generic illustrations.
- They should not be used indiscriminately and without reference to a qualified legal advisor as some of them may not be appropriate to your given situation.

APPENDIX A

Draft covering letter

[Company]

[Contact name]

[Address]

[Date]

Dear Sir/Madam,

Re: Request for information for **[describe PRODUCT or SERVICE]**.

We are currently reviewing our requirements with a number of present and potential suppliers.

The contract for the provision of such **[PRODUCT or SERVICE]** is estimated to be valued at around $X per annum.

If you are interested in being considered for this process, please complete the attached questionnaire and forward your responses no later than **[date]** to:

[Principal's delegate]

[Principal's address]

Your responses to the attached request for information will help us to better understand how your company could best serve our needs. Following this stage, potential partners selected will be supplied with a tender package and invited to submit a bid.

Please note that the submission of information requested herein does not necessarily mean you will be invited to Tender or that you will necessarily be notified of our decision in this regard.

Should you have any questions, please do not hesitate to contact **[name of Principal's delegate]** on **[telephone number** or **email address**].

Yours faithfully

[Delegate's name]

[For and on behalf of the Principal]

APPENDIX B

REQUEST FOR INFORMATION (RFI)

I. GENERAL INFORMATION

Company's legal name: ....

Parent company name: ....

Share capital: ....

Number of employees: ....

Head office address: ....

Date and place of incorporation:..

Person to contact following this enquiry, in case of an invitation to tender:

Name:..

Position: ....

Tel: ....

Fax: ....

E-mail:..

Company's legal status *(please tick the appropriate box below)*

- Public limited company ☐
- Private company ☐
- Joint venture ☐
- Other (specify) ☐

➪ ***Please enclose an official organisation chart of the company showing subsidiaries and divisions.***

II. PRODUCTS/SERVICES

Please indicate the products or services that you might be in a position to supply to us. Attach a schedule if necessary.

III. HISTORY

If you have or have had dealings with any of our subsidiaries, namely **[list names of relevant subsidiaries]**, please provide us with information in a summary in format below:

Name of subsidiary	Goods or services provided	Contract turnover in 2002	Contract turnover in 2001	Contract turnover in 2000

Please list the names of people you are dealing with/have previously dealt with from our organisation.

....

IV. FINANCIAL INFORMATION

Please complete particulars of your turnover and net profit results for the specified years:

	2002	2001	2000
Turnover			
Net profit			

➪ ***Please provide us with a copy of your latest audited financial statements including a balance sheet and a profit and loss statement for the most recent financial year.***

V. GEOGRAPHICAL COVERAGE

Please provide a list of all your distribution centres (providing details of their geographical coverage). Kindly follow the format below:

Distribution Centre Name	City Area (m^2)	Integrated *(please tick)*	Subcontracted *(please tick)*

Distribution/transport vehicles:
Owned/leased ☐ Number:...
Subcontracted ☐ Number:...
if subcontracted, give names and address of subcontractors:

Name	Address

VI. QUALITY SYSTEMS AND CERTIFICATIONS

Please provide any relevant information concerning your current quality systems (whether officially certified or otherwise)

➪ ***Please provide a copy of your quality manual.***

VII. INVOICING AND REFERENCES

Is your invoicing system centralised? (please tick)

Yes ☐ No ☐

Please provide a list of your most significant business references indicating the contract turnover with these referees.

Please provide the information in the format shown below:

Referee's name	Contract turnover amount for the last financial year

➪ ***Please provide a copy of your usual trading terms.***

APPENDIX C

Tender Form

Number [123456]

[PRODUCT/S and/or SERVICES CATEGORY]

[Tenderer's name] hereby submits its Tender for the supply of **[product/s or services]**.

The Tenderer hereby accepts and undertakes to be bound by the Conditions of Tender.

Attached to and forming part of the Tender are the following documents:

— Conditions of Contract Form
— Pricing Schedule
— Products and Service Schedule
— Key Performance Indicators Form
— Quality Assurance Form

This Tender is an open offer capable of acceptance by the Principal and shall remain open for acceptance for a minimum period of ninety (90) days from the Closing Date during which time it cannot be withdrawn by the Tenderer.

All correspondence and enquiries in relation to the Tender may be addressed to:

[Tenderer's representative]

[Full address]

[Telephone numbers]

[Fax number]

[E-mail address]

Signed for and behalf of the Tenderer by its authorised officers:

Signature: ....
[Date]

Signature: ....
[Date]

APPENDIX D

SAMPLE CONDITIONS OF TENDER

1. LODGEMENT OF TENDER

(a) The Tender shall be delivered by hand or by courier and placed into the Tender Box by no later than 4.00 pm on the Closing Date.

(b) The Tender shall be sealed in an envelope or in a suitable package, clearly marked with the Tender Number and title as shown on the front cover on the Tender Document.

(c) The Tenderer shall ensure that its Tender is lodged in the Tender Box by 4.00 pm on the Closing Date.

(d) Tenders lodged by post, facsimile, email or any other means will not be accepted.

2. LATE TENDERS

(a) Any Tender lodged in the Tender Box for whatever reason after 4.00 pm on the Closing Date is a Late Tender.

(b) Late Tenders will be disqualified and excluded from consideration.

(c) It is the Tenderer's obligation to ensure that the Tender documents reach the Tender Box prior to 4.00 pm on the Closing Date.

3. ACCEPTANCE OF TENDERS

(a) The Principal is not bound to accept the lowest, or any, Tender and may reject any or all Tenders submitted.

(b) Unless otherwise stated in the Request for Tender, offers may be for all or part of the requirement and may be accepted by the Principal either wholly or in part.

(c) The Principal may at its absolute discretion reject any tender as invalid, which does not conform with the Tender document.

(d) No Tender is accepted until an official notification is so despatched by the Principal to the successful tenderer/s.

(e) The acceptance of any Tender (or part thereof) by the Principal shall be conditional upon the successful tenderer executing a formal instrument of contract. Failure by the successful tenderer to duly execute and return the instrument of contract, within the time limit specified in the Letter of Acceptance (time being of the essence), will result in the automatic withdrawal of the Principal's acceptance of the tender.

OR

(e) The successful Tenderer will be notified in writing of the acceptance of its Tender. The notification of the acceptance of Tender will create a contract between the parties on the basis of the successful Tenderer's Tender and the Contract Documents. The successful Tenderer must execute and return to the Principal a formal agreement in the form of the Contract Documents, as amended by the insertion of any details which Tenderers are required to include in Tenders within 7 days of its receipt from the Principal.

[EXPLANATORY NOTE: The use of the first version of sub-clause (e) shown above may be optional, as it may allow a tenderer to withdraw if it refuses to sign the contract. In some circumstances, a Principal may consider this to be inappropriate. As an alternative, the second sub-clause (e) may be used]

4. CONDITIONS OF CONTRACT

Tenders shall be deemed to have been made on the basis of and to incorporate the Conditions of Contract, a copy of which has been made available to the Tenderer.

5. **NON-CONFORMING TENDERS**

(a) Tenders submitted as alternative Tenders or made subject to conditions other than the Conditions of Contract shall in all cases arising be clearly marked "**NON-CONFORMING TENDER**".

(b) Any printed "Conditions of Contract" shown on or attached to a Tenderer's letter or quotation form will not be binding on the Principal in the event of a contract being awarded unless the Tender is marked as a Non-Conforming Tender.

(c) The Principal may at its absolute discretion reject any Non-Conforming Tender as invalid.

6. **TENDERED PRICES**

(a) Unless otherwise indicated, the Tender prices shall be expressed in Australian dollars (A$) and shall include any and all freight and delivery charges, unloading, packing, marking and all applicable levies, duties, taxes and charges.

(b) Any charge not stated in the Tender as being additional, will not be allowed as a charge against any transaction under any resultant contract.

7. **VALIDITY**

(a) All Tenders shall be open offers capable of acceptance by the Principal and shall remain open for acceptance for a minimum period of ninety (90) days from the Closing Date.

(b) No Tender shall be withdrawn by the Tenderer without the prior written consent of the Principal.

8. **PRICE BASIS**

(a) Tenderers **must** state the price basis applicable to the goods offered.

(b) <u>Preference will be given to offers that are firm for the entire term of the Contract</u>.

9. **VALUE FOR MONEY POLICY**

(a) The Principal has adopted a value for money approach to all of its procurement activities to ensure the best possible return from all the Principal's expenditure on goods and/or services, recognising that this may not necessarily amount to purchasing at the lowest price to specification.

(b) As such, the "value for money" approach embraces the total cost of the product or service over the life of the requirement, fitness for purpose, timely delivery, and local support. It also involves an assessment of the wider benefits it may contribute to other objectives in areas such as business and industry development, environmental protection, energy conservation, etc

10. QUALITY ASSURANCE PROVISIONS

(a) Preference will be given to Tenderers that have current Quality Assurance programs in place except where their Tenders do not, in the Principal's opinion, represent value for money, or do not otherwise adequately satisfy the requirements of the tender documents.

(b) A Tender not complying with the Quality Assurance requirement but which, in the Principal's opinion, does give value for money, may be accepted in this case.

(c) Tenderers are required to include with their Tender submissions a photocopy of their relevant Certificate of Registration and Schedule issued by a recognised certifying body.

(d) The Tenderer shall have in place and maintain management practices and processes that ensure the goods or services are provided in accordance with the specified requirements detailed in this tender and to the complete satisfaction of the Principal.

11. IDENTITY OF TENDERER

(a) The Tenderer shall be the person, persons, corporation or corporations named as the Tenderer in the OFFER BY TENDERER at the end of these conditions.

(b) Where the Tenderer is a partnership, joint venture or consortium, the full legal names and respective percentage interest in the partnership, joint venture or consortium must be provided. Where such information is not provided, the Principal shall consider the Tender to be a Non-Conforming Tender.

(c) Upon acceptance of the Tender, the Tenderer shall become the Contractor.

12. NO ASSIGNMENT

This tender is personal to, not assignable or transferable by the Tenderer or the legal personal representative of the Tenderer without the prior written consent of the Principal.

13. OWNERSHIP OF TENDER RESPONSES

All documents, materials, articles and information submitted by the Tenderer as part of, or in support of a Tender are provided free of charge and shall become, upon submission, the absolute property of the Principal and will not be returned to the Tenderer at the conclusion of the Tender process.

14. CONFIDENTIALITY

(a) The content of all offers will be treated as "commercial-in-confidence".

(b) The successful tenderer shall sign the Principal's standard form of Confidentiality Agreement (a copy of which has been provided to all Tenderers) as a condition of this Contract.

15. FORMAT OF TENDER RESPONSE

(a) The Tenderer shall provide an original hardcopy of its tender, so marked and bound plus three (3) complete copies of its original Tender on a Microsoft Office 2000 compatible compact disk (CD).

(b) Tender responses **must** be submitted in the following format. Failure to respond accordingly may result in a Tender being rejected.

(i) Tenderers must address each and every section of the Request for Tender using the same numbering sequence as the Request for Tender.

(ii) Information in support of, or explanation of, the above form of answers should follow immediately after the answer.

16. CLARIFICATION OF TENDER DOCUMENT

If the Tenderer is in doubt as to the true meaning of any part of the Tender document, it shall notify the Principal's Contract Administrator nominated on the front of the Tender document and obtain clarification prior to lodging its Tender. The Principal will not be liable for any claim due to any mis-interpretation by the Tenderer.

17. NO COLLATERAL CONTRACT

The submission of a Tender by a Contractor will not give rise to any contract governing, or in any way concerning, the Tender process, or any aspect of the Tender process, for this Contract. The Principal expressly disclaims any intention to enter into any such contract.

18. EVALUATION CRITERIA

(a) The Tender evaluation panel will evaluate Tenders in accordance with evaluation criteria listed (in order of importance) in Schedule 1.

(b) The Principal will award the Tender by applying the Best Value Principles. In applying the Best Value Principles, the Principal will have regard to (if that is relevant — needs to be defined) the report prepared by the Tender evaluation panel and any other factors which it considers relevant.

19. POST-TENDER SUBMISSIONS

(a) The Principal may require a Contractor to submit additional information concerning its Tender or to personally discuss its Tender before any Tender is accepted.

(b) Should a Contractor fail to —

(i) submit the additional information so required by; or

(ii) attend personally to discuss its Tender at —

the date and time stipulated by the Principal, its Tender may not be further considered.

20. RECTIFICATION OF ERRORS AND OMISSIONS

The Principal reserves the right to:

(a) check Tenders for errors and omissions;

(b) by agreement with a Tenderer, amend a Tender price or rate submitted by a Tenderer to remedy the effect of any errors or omissions in the calculation of the Tender price or rate; and

(c) by agreement with a Tenderer, otherwise amend the Tender of the Tenderer to remedy the effect of any errors or omissions.

21. GUARANTEE

Tenderers are advised that the Principal may accept a Tender on condition that a guarantee in respect of the Contractor's obligations under the Contract, in the form of the Deed of Guarantee annexed to the Contract Documents, is executed by persons or bodies corporate specified in the Principal's acceptance.

22. CANVASSING

(a) Contractors must not approach, or request any other person to approach any officer of the Principal to solicit support for their Tenders or otherwise seek to influence the outcome of the Tender process.

(b) The Tender of any Contractor which engages in conduct prohibited under this clause may not be considered by the Principal.

23. STATUTORY DECLARATION

A statutory declaration in the form of the annexure must be made by a person authorised to make such a declaration on behalf of the Contractor and submitted with its Tender.

APPENDIX E

Statutory Declaration

I, ...do solemnly and sincerely declare that:

Definitions

1. In this Statutory Declaration:

   Bidders means any Tenderers for the Contract and includes the Tenderer;

   the Contract means the contract that the Tender Conditions to which this Statutory Declaration is a schedule pertains;

   Industry Association means any organisation of which Bidders are members;

   the Tenderer means **[insert name of company, other body corporate, firm, or individual]**

   ....

   ....; and

   Tender Price means the amount indicated by a Bidder as the lowest amount for which that Bidder is prepared to perform the Contract.

***Introduction**

2. I am the Tenderer and make this declaration on my own behalf.

***Introduction**

2. 2.1 I hold the position of **[insert Managing Director or other title]** of the Tenderer and am duly authorised by the Tenderer to make this declaration on its behalf.

2.2 I make this declaration on behalf of the Tenderer and on behalf of myself.

[*Delete alternative which is not applicable]

No knowledge of Tender Prices

3. Prior to the Tenderer submitting its Tender for the Contract, neither the Tenderer, nor any of its employees or agents, had knowledge of the Tender Price, or proposed Tender Price, of any other Bidder who submitted, or of any person, company, other body corporate or firm that proposed to submit, a Tender for the Contract.

Disclosure of Tender Price

4. Prior to the close of Tenders for the Contract, neither the Tenderer, nor any of its employees or agents, disclosed the Tenderer's Tender Price to:

   4.1 any other Bidder who submitted a Tender for the Contract;

   4.2 any person, company, other body corporate or firm proposing to submit a Tender for the Contract; or

   4.3 any person or organisation connected or associated with a Bidder, person, company, other body corporate or firm of a kind referred to in clauses 4.1 or 4.2.

Provision of Information

5. Neither the Tenderer, nor any of its employees or agents, has provided information, except for a published catalogue or price list normally made available to customers of the Tenderer, to:

   5.1 any other Bidder who has submitted a Tender for the Contract;

   5.2 any person, company, other body corporate or firm proposing to submit a Tender for the Contract; or

   5.3 any other person, company, other body corporate or firm for the purpose of assisting in the preparation of a Tender for the Contract.

Genuine Competition

6. The Tenderer is genuinely competing for the Contract.

Industry Association Agreements

7. Neither the Tenderer, nor any of its employees or agents, has entered into any contract, agreement, arrangement or understanding, other than as disclosed to the Principal in the Tenderer's Tender, that the successful Bidder for the Contract will pay any money to, or provide any other benefit or other financial advantage to, an Industry Association in respect of the Contract.

Unsuccessful Tenderers' Fees

8. Neither the Tenderer, nor any of its employees or agents, has entered into any contract, agreement, arrangement or understanding that the successful Bidder for the Contract will pay any money to, or provide any other benefit or other financial advantage to, any other Bidder who or which unsuccessfully tendered for the Contract.

Qualifications to Tenders

9. Neither the Tenderer, nor any of its employees or agents, has entered into any contract, agreement, arrangement or understanding that Bidders for the Contract would include an identical or similar condition or qualification in their Tenders for the Contract.

Conflict of Interest

10. Neither the Tenderer, nor any of its employees or agents has a potential or actual conflict of interest between performing the Contract and any other interest.

I acknowledge that this declaration is true and correct and I make it in the belief that a person making a false declaration is liable to the penalties of perjury.

DECLARED at ....
in the State of New South Wales

on ....20 ....

Before Me: ....

Signature:...

Full Name:...

Address:...

Qualifications:...

[Insert details of the basis on which you are entitled to witness a Statutory Declaration under the relevant section of the Oaths Act or Evidence Act in the State or place in which the declaration is made (eg as a justice of the peace or solicitor etc).]

INDEX

Corporate Legal Education & Development (CLED) can assist your organisation

The author of this series, **Frank Adoranti**, is the principal of the specialised legal risk management consultancy ***Corporate Legal Education & Development (CLED).***

CLED is a specialist provider of legal risk management consultancy services to multinational corporations worldwide. Some of the range of services includes:

- legal audits (legal risk health checks);
- devising contract management solutions;
- other legal risk management advice;
- assistance in negotiating major contracts and deals;
- reviewing tenders and advising on major contract bids;
- specialised business consulting activities;
- formulating business and corporate policy;
- devising codes of conduct;
- crisis management planning and events;
- mergers and acquisitions;
- corporate restructuring;
- speaking at corporate functions and conventions;
- conducting training and seminars for management.

CLED provides such services in virtually any country in Asia, Europe or North America.

CLED is also able to assist you in working with the publisher for bulk and/or customised orders of the **Managers Guide Series** of books for your organisation.

To enquire about the possibility of having **Frank Adoranti** working with your organisation, please either:

- **fax** back this form to ***+612 8824 9308***

or

- **email** your enquiry to: ***frank@adoranti.com***

Name: ....

Organisation: ....

Country: ....

Title: ....

Email: ....

Tel: ....

Nature of enquiry: ....

....

....

Desired method of contact:

- Please phone me to discuss
- Please email me